FRAUD WATCH

A guide for business

Typeset by J&L Composition Ltd, Filey, North Yorkshire
Printed in Great Britain by Bell and Bain Ltd, Glasgow

FRAUD WATCH

A guide for business

IAN HUNTINGTON and DAVID DAVIES

KPMG Forensic Accounting

The Institute of Chartered Accountants
in England and Wales
Gloucester House
399 Silbury Boulevard
Central Milton Keynes
MK9 2HL
Tel: 0908 248000

British Library Cataloguing-in-Publication Data
A catalogue record for this book is available from the British Library

ISBN 1 85355 5207

Throughout this book the male pronoun is used to cover references to both the male and female.

Foreword

'Power tends to corrupt, and absolute power corrupts absolutely.'

Acton drew his famous conclusion a hundred years ago. Nothing changes today, when major investigations are reported in the United States, the United Kingdom, Germany, France, Italy, Spain, Hong Kong, Venezuela, Japan and Korea into cases whose consistent theme is corruption and the abuse of power.

Fraud and its roots – greed and arrogance – are human nature. As business people, we must recognise fraud as a permanent risk, a risk we must take action to manage.

It is a commonplace that we live in a world of accelerating change. But change is creating greater incentives for fraud and greater opportunities to defraud. Today's empowered manager is offered higher rewards if he succeeds, but swift dismissal if he does not. What greater encouragement is there to manipulate the financial statements by which success or failure are measured?

At the same time, opportunities are being created by change at both high and detailed levels. For example, economic and regulatory changes in Russia seem to have led to what the English have since 1720 called *bubbles* (*Ponzi schemes* in American parlance). More mundanely, in a short time the fax has been transformed from a high tech gadget to a routine business tool; how many companies appreciate how easily faxes can be forged, so that they risk relying on crucial documentation which is not authentic?

There is no shortage of advice about fraud. Fraud has become an industry – and not just for fraudsters. Academics study it. Investigators investigate it. Lawyers litigate on it. But the industry is built on managing the consequences of fraud rather than on preventing fraud. Publications reflect the same pattern. Each major scandal has generated its instant biography of the villain and the stories of the fraud – but little by way of practical advice on what business should do to manage fraud risk from day to day.

Our book is an exception to that rule. The Auditing Committee of the Institute of Chartered Accountants in England and Wales felt that business people and their auditors needed practical help and advice on fraud prevention and asked KPMG to prepare this book. It draws on the practical experience of KPMG's London office (in particular our fraud investigation group), giving many examples and providing realistic advice on the types of risks that companies may encounter.

Michael Fowle
Senior Partner KPMG South East Region

August 1994

PREFACE

Over the years some elaborate theories and classifications of corporate fraud have been developed. Criminologists and academics on both sides of the Atlantic have undertaken research into the possible motives and psychological attributes of fraudsters. Interesting though many of these studies are, it is often quite difficult for those responsible for managing the risk of fraud in companies to relate the findings to their particular business circumstances. In short, there is a lack of clear, concise and practical advice.

Our aim in this guide is to help businesses to manage the risk of fraud more effectively and to identify the warning signs – the red flags. The main part of the guide is therefore given over to a detailed examination of the frauds which commonly occur in companies and how they may be detected and prevented.

Fraud may occur at any level in a company. A few frauds are more likely to be committed by senior management and others by more junior staff but the majority may be committed by staff at every level of a company and in a wide variety of circumstances. We have not tried, therefore, to categorise management and employee frauds by seniority.

We have also not sought to categorise the frauds into 'serious fraud' and 'not so serious fraud'. Any fraud perpetrated by directors or senior managers will cause concern. However, whether it is regarded as 'serious fraud' or not depends largely on the amounts involved and the particular circumstances in which the fraud occurred. Of course, over the years there have been a few major cases involving corruption on a massive scale at main board level. It is not the purpose of this book to analyse these major cases because they are not representative of the core risks facing most companies and in any case books and public inquiry reports have already been written about most of them. Nevertheless, certain elements of those cases are similar to frauds which may occur in companies more generally and to that extent they are dealt with in this guide.

We see the guide as being of primary use to businesses seeking to manage the risk of fraud. We hope the guide will be useful to directors and senior managers, and also to internal auditors. The guide may also be valuable in appraising risk in other businesses which companies may acquire. Many of the issues raised in the guide are also applicable to organisations in the public sector. We have highlighted in Chapter 4 certain frauds which are especially prevalent in that sector.

The legal consequences of fraud are not covered as this subject has been dealt with fully elsewhere. Guidance on legal aspects is available in Ian

Huntington's book *Fraud: Prevention and Detection* and the legal textbooks referred to in the list of further reading at the back of the guide.

We have also not dealt with many aspects of commercial crime – e.g., fraud *by* companies against their customers or their competitors or abuse of the environment. This is a large subject worthy of a separate book in itself. Fraud investigation is also outside the scope of the guide. Our main focus is on the risks of fraud and fraud prevention.

There is an argument that books of this type increase the risk of fraud by providing potential fraudsters with the knowledge and the skills to commit frauds that might otherwise never have taken place. The premise on which this guide is based is that if businesses are to protect themselves against fraud, it is essential that they understand how they may be defrauded and the risks they are running. It is only with this understanding that they can take appropriate steps to reduce those risks. We have omitted certain operational details where we believe these would be prejudicial to the interests of companies.

The authors would like to thank the following for their contributions to the guide:

- Miller Ross, partner in KPMG Peat Marwick, London, and Malcolm Marshall, senior manager in KPMG Computer Audit, who wrote Chapter 6 on computer risks and the section on computer security in Chapter 7, David Eastwood, senior manager in KPMG Forensic Accounting, London, for his input to Chapters 2, 3 and 7, and Ian Dewar, partner in KPMG Peat Marwick, London, who contributed material to the section on dealing room fraud in Chapter 5;
- Ernst & Young for their permission to refer to their *Fraud 92* survey in Chapter 1;
- the Joint Money Laundering Steering Group for their permission to use material on money laundering in Chapters 4 and 5 and in the appendices based on parts of the guidance notes for mainstream banking, lending and deposit taking activities, for wholesale institutional and private client investment business and for insurance and retail investment products, issued in October 1993;
- the Audit Commission for permission to refer to extracts from the *Survey of Computer Fraud and Abuse* in Chapter 6;
- the British Standards Institute for their permission to reproduce an extract from *A Code of Practice for Information Security Management* in Chapter 7;
- the Institute of Business Ethics for their permission to reproduce the example statement of business principles and code of business ethics in Chapter 7;
- Butterworth & Co (Publishers) Ltd, London for their permission to reprint certain examples first used by Ian Huntington in his book *Fraud: Prevention and Detection*, published by Butterworths in 1992; and

- Tony Groag and other members of the internal audit department at The British Petroleum Company plc for consultations early in the development of the guide.

Finally, we thank our colleagues in KPMG Forensic Accounting, London for their assistance and Anna Ball and Teresa Morley for their dedication and support in typing the original text of the guide.

Ian Huntington August 1994
David Davies

Ian Huntington is Head of Fraud Investigation and David Davies is a Senior Manager in KPMG Forensic Accounting, London. KPMG Forensic Accounting has 90 specialist partners and staff in the UK assigned full time to investigating fraud and assisting with the litigation process.

In the last five years KPMG has investigated cases with sums at risk ranging from a few thousand pounds to over £1 billion, including investigations for major companies, government agencies and regulators. In addition, KPMG provides fraud awareness training and risk management programmes to corporates and regulators worldwide.

Contents

1 INTRODUCTION

Fraud: a growing problem

Nobody, after BCCI, Barlow Clowes, Milken and the savings and loan frauds in the United States – and certain infamous alleged frauds still sub-judice – will dissent from the proposition that:

> *'fraud and deceit abound in these days more than in former times'.*

This was said nearly 400 years ago in 1602, by Sir Edward Coke, a leading lawyer and politician of the Elizabethan era. We are not dealing with a new problem.

Most recent surveys show that fraud is a growing problem. For example, the KPMG Fraud Barometer, an index of reported fraud in the United Kingdom, indicates that fraud has increased significantly in recent years:

Table 1: ***The KPMG Fraud Barometer***

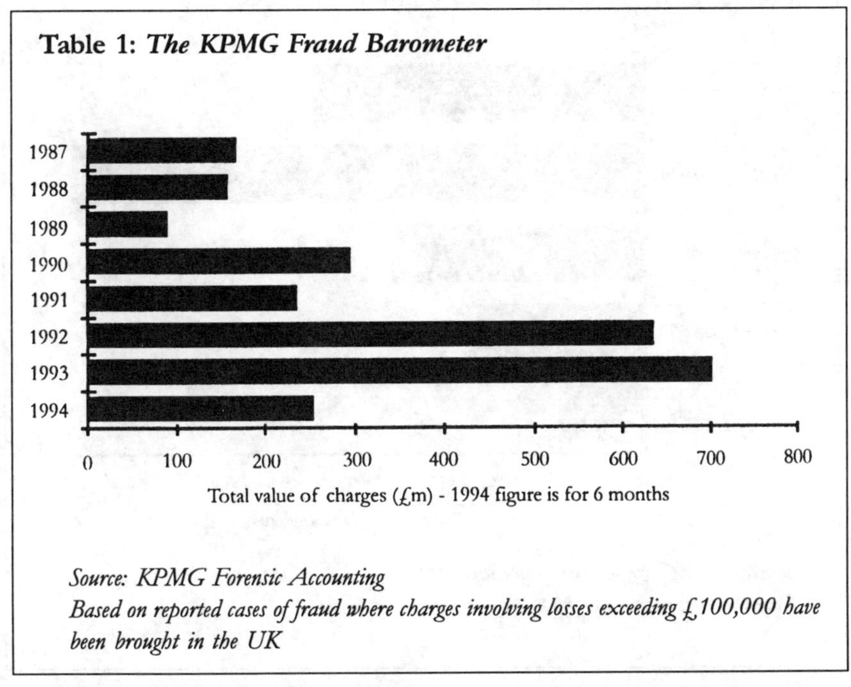

Source: KPMG Forensic Accounting
Based on reported cases of fraud where charges involving losses exceeding £100,000 have been brought in the UK

Other recent surveys show similar trends. For example, a survey based on questionnaires completed by senior executives from 100 British companies, indicated that:

- 30 per cent of companies had reported a fraud of over £50,000 and 24 per cent a fraud of over £250,000 in the last two years;
- one third of companies had suffered but not reported a fraud; and
- 62 per cent of companies believed that fraud had become much more common over the last five years*.

Fraud is a problem in other major industrialised nations too. Recently KPMG conducted fraud surveys in the United States and five other countries internationally. In the United States, for example, 52 per cent of respondents believed that fraud was an increasing problem. 77 per cent of respondents reported having experienced fraud during the past year, with 18 per cent of those companies having lost more than US$1 million.

However, given the reluctance of companies to publicise their experience of fraud and the low level of criminal prosecutions that actually take place, the real incidence of fraud is certain to be much higher than that shown by the KPMG Fraud Barometer and the other surveys.

Table 2: ***Cost of fraud to United States companies***

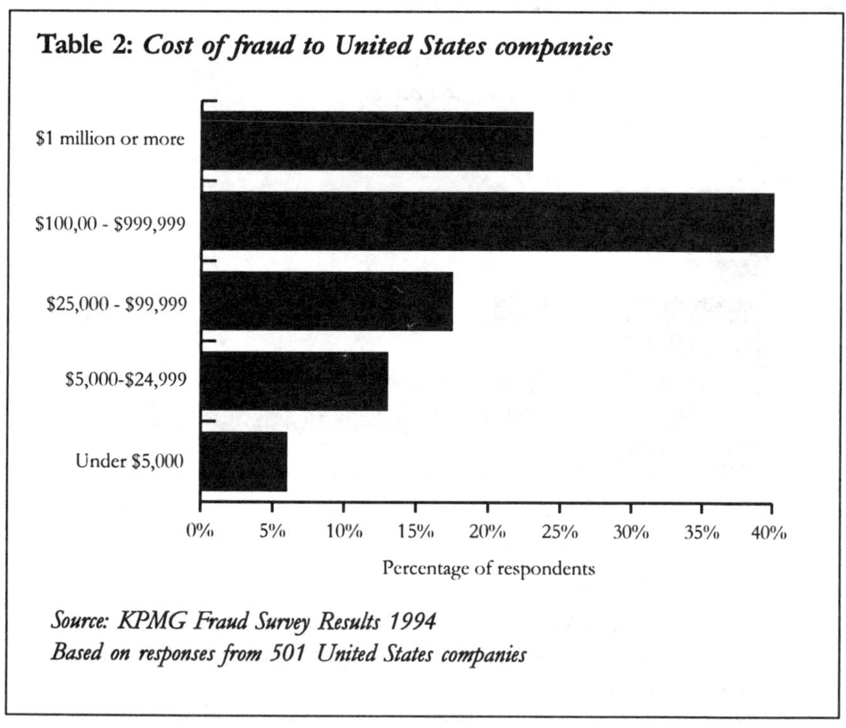

Source: KPMG Fraud Survey Results 1994
Based on responses from 501 United States companies

* *Fraud 92* survey conducted by Ernst & Young in collaboration with the leading criminologist Professor Michael Levi.

What is fraud?

English law does not define fraud. However, Buckley J's description in *Re London and Globe Finance Ltd* encapsulates the two key elements: *'to defraud is to deprive by deceit'*. This description underlines the two essential elements in any fraud:

- deception or concealment; and
- deprival or loss to the victim.

In this guide we concentrate on the corporate victim: the ways in which companies may suffer loss due to fraud.

A simple analysis of fraud would classify fraud into two main categories:

- removal of funds or assets from the business; and
- misrepresentation of the financial position of the business.

Removal of funds or assets includes theft of cash from bank accounts, removal of other assets such as stock, manipulation of the company's relationships with suppliers or customers, overstatement of claims, undisclosed creation of credit and the assumption of liabilities. Misrepresentation of the company's financial position includes false accounting such as the omission, misrecording or manipulation of the company's accounting records.

The criminal law defines by statute certain specific offences, the most common being theft under s1 of the Theft Act 1968, obtaining property by deception under s15 of the Theft Act 1968, and false accounting under s17 of the Theft Act 1968; carrying on business with the intent to defraud under s458 of the Companies Act 1985 and the common law offence of conspiracy to defraud. However, as noted in the preface, we do not intend to cover the legal consequences of fraud as this subject has been dealt with fully in other books.

Managing the risk

Any company is at risk of fraud and it is the directors' task to manage that risk professionally, applying to it the same techniques which should be applied to all business problems: analysing the scope and scale of the risk, developing a strategy to minimise the risk, and implementing the strategy.

But managing the risk is difficult. The whole point about fraud is that it is plausible. Fraudsters are expert at manipulating people and documents and at covering their tracks. The appearance may therefore be normal but the reality quite different. Deception is key to any fraud.

Many companies tend to narrow their field of vision by looking only at accounting procedures and controls rather than the specific risks of fraud which the business faces. They do not take account of the whole spectrum of risk. The fraudster is not only interested in the straightforward, and often highly visible, theft of cash but also:

- the ability of a business to generate credit, for example, through loans, guarantees or trade credit;
- the power to commit the business to contracts, to accept liabilities and to approve invoices;
- contingent assets and rights and commercial secrets; and
- the ability to control resources and accounting records under separate legal ownership, for example relating to pension or trust funds and client accounts.

The spectrum of risk

CASH	CREDIT	COMMITMENT	CONTINGENCIES	CONTROL

Accounting procedures and controls may give a false sense of security. They may operate quite differently in theory than in practice. Fraudsters are opportunists who take advantage of temporary weaknesses or unnoticed gaps between the apparent strength and the real effectiveness of controls. For example, physically or culturally remote locations, informal networks and disparities between personal authority and corporate status can weaken controls and give the fraudster the opportunity he or she requires.

It is important to appreciate the nature of the risk and to remember that it is people, not businesses or systems, who commit fraud.

Some companies have taken special measures to counter fraud, for example by appointing security officers or setting up dedicated fraud investigation units. Sometimes these units deal only with fraud which is reported to them and do not play a proactive role in helping directors and managers to manage the risk of fraud in the business. The focus also may be only on external threats (for example in banks, cheque fraud and credit card frauds), overlooking what may be the greater threat, the enemy within. The

KPMG Fraud Barometer indicates that more than half of corporate fraud is committed by, or in collusion with, management and employees.

Other companies focus on the specialised frauds affecting their particular industry (for example, airline ticket fraud in airlines) but ignore more general types of fraud, such as procurement fraud, which may be a significant risk for any company in relation to major capital projects, maintenance, design or consultancy contracts.

The major frauds reported in the press tend to divert attention from what are, for most companies, the core risks. Press reports are often sensational in style and do not draw out the wider lessons for companies generally. Companies may therefore believe that 'it could not possibly happen to us' and overlook the risk that a slightly different, but equally devastating fraud, could occur in their own business.

Certain types of fraud attract a disproportionate amount of publicity. For example, advance fee fraud (see Chapter 4) has attracted a good deal of attention in recent years. Undoubtedly advance fee fraud is a significant threat for certain businesses but it is only one of at least 10 significant threats to companies in the procurement and purchasing area – and some of the more significant threats may be management and employee frauds, not external frauds.

Fraud Watch: our aim

In Chapter 2 we examine the factors which may make a company more susceptible to fraud. We then go on to look at the possible motives and attributes of fraudsters and some of the techniques of deception they use in Chapter 3.

The main part of the guide (Chapters 4 and 5) is devoted to a detailed examination of the key risks which companies typically face. Of course, the risk of fraud always needs to be considered in relation to particular companies and particular business circumstances. No checklist can cover all the frauds which may occur. However, there are many common themes, frauds which occur again and again, albeit in slightly different forms. These frauds are best understood in the context of particular business cycles. We look at sales, purchases, inventory and cash and payment systems. We identify the points in the respective cycles at which the risk of fraud is greatest. We also look at frauds in other areas, such as payroll, company car schemes, intercompany and suspense accounts, share support schemes, misuse of government funding and the misuse of pension fund assets.

Each industry has its own more specialised types of fraud, for example in the motor trade 'clocking' (turning odometers back) or 'ringing' (giving crashed or stolen cars new identities). As already noted, we do not attempt to cover all of these more specialised types of fraud. They are usually well known in each industry. The financial sector is different though. Due to the complexity of business there are a very large number of such specialised frauds and we therefore devote the whole of Chapter 5 to the specialised risks in this sector. We look at banking, investment business and insurance in turn.

We distinguish between internal frauds (i.e., those committed by management and employees) and external frauds. Sometimes the distinction is far from clear, for example where collusion is involved, but in most cases the risks are quite distinct. We illustrate the various types of frauds with examples. The examples given in the main text are set out in more detail in the Digest of Cases at the back of the guide and further examples are given to illustrate some of the variations and to demonstrate the range of businesses in which the frauds may occur.

Certain types of fraud are outside the scope of the guide, in particular:

- counterfeit product frauds;
- specialised frauds relating to the use of products in particular industries;
- tax frauds;
- bankruptcy frauds;
- credit card frauds; and
- franchise frauds.

In Chapter 6 we deal with the specific risks associated with the use of computers. There are a few types of fraud which relate specifically to the computer system itself, for example manipulation of programs and hacking. However, most frauds are not 'computer frauds' as such. The computer is the medium through which transactions are processed. What the computer does is to increase the risk of certain types of fraud, for example through weak access controls, shortcomings in programs, changes in the segregation of duties or the ease with which funds may be transferred.

Chapter 7 is devoted to fraud prevention. We examine the key elements in developing an effective fraud prevention strategy while in the final chapter we reflect on some of the broader issues affecting business today and the fight against fraud.

2 INDICATORS OF FRAUD

Introduction

When fraud is investigated factors often emerge which, at least with the benefit of hindsight, should have put the company on notice that all was not well. These factors made the company more susceptible to fraud. Assessing these factors is only part of the risk appraisal process. There may of course be more specific warning signs of particular types of fraud, such as those described in Chapters 4 and 5 of this guide. However, this does not reduce the need to consider the broader issues. It is important not to become lost in the detail and hence fail to see the big picture.

None of the factors discussed in this chapter is likely on its own to indicate fraud. However, where there is a combination of several factors there will usually be a high level of risk. There are many ways of looking at these risk factors. For the purposes of this chapter we group them into four categories:

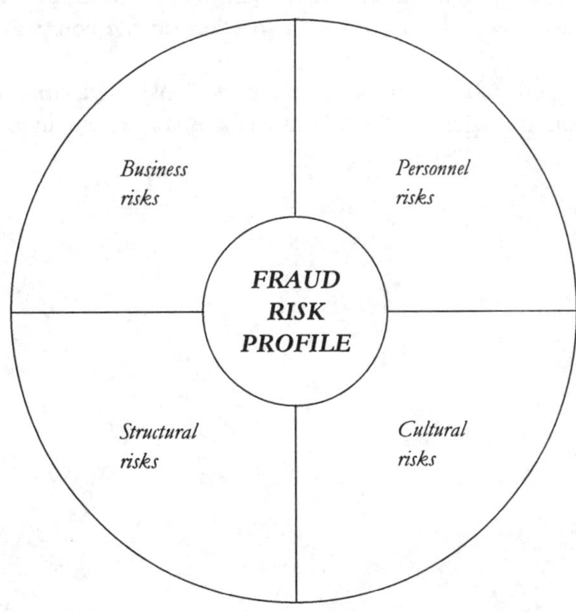

Before we discuss the various factors in detail we should emphasise that the risk profile of any company may change from low to high risk very quickly. For example, changes in personnel or in systems can result in a significant change to the risk profile. Similarly, economic factors or changes in market conditions may increase the risk of fraud. Structural changes in a business may also create new risks, for example through acquisitions, disposals or reorganisations.

Set out below are some examples of the ways in which change may affect the risk profile of a company:

- personnel changes – changes in senior personnel may affect the culture of a company; changes in reporting lines, in the segregation of duties or the competence of personnel may undermine the apparent controls;
- computer systems changes may create unnoticed gaps in controls – for example a major company, when streamlining its computer system, unwittingly allowed 10,000 extra users access to its financial accounting system;
- acquisitions may create unforeseen risks – for example, the profits forming the basis of an earnout may be manipulated by the vendors bearing certain expenses personally or hiding costs in accounts which are reviewed infrequently; disgruntled ex-directors of recently acquired companies, who remain in the business, may divert business to rival companies owned by them;
- disposals may result in additional risk, for example there may be weak controls over the sales of assets which result in less than full value being achieved; reorganisations and redundancies may result in low morale and employees may seek to avenge themselves on the company.

Whenever major change in a business is considered, the risk of fraud should be on the agenda. We discuss risk management in more detail in Chapter 7.

Personnel risks

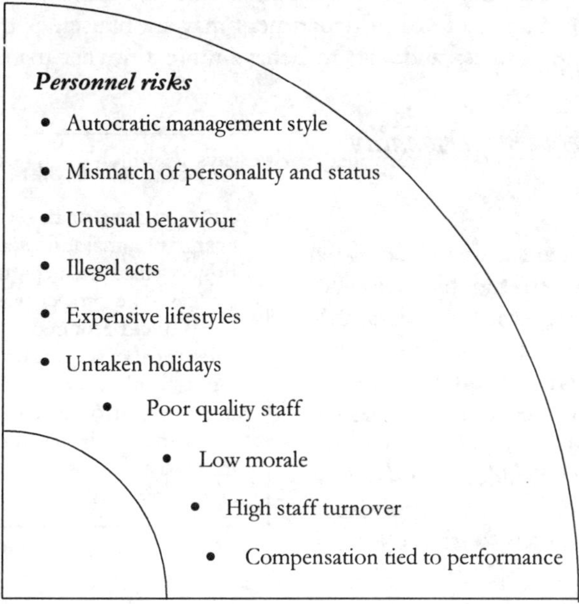

Autocratic management style

Companies take their character from the chief executive or board. A cut corner approach to business by senior executives may lead to a cut corner approach to financial controls throughout the organisation.

As is well known, in certain major reported frauds overriding dominance by a chairman or chief executive has been an important factor. But does strong leadership and charisma necessarily lead to a problem? The lack of such qualities may itself be a cause for concern. The key is how such power is exercised. Situations which may cause concern are:

- transactions which are known only to one or two directors;
- no meaningful debate of business issues at board level;
- frequent override of senior managers' authority; and
- obsessive secrecy where such behaviour is not justified.

A related problem arises where a sole director has exclusive control over a significant part of the business, for example certain overseas operations, with little or no independent review of those activities by anyone else at board or senior management level. This might occur, for example, where a group finance director is prevented from examining closely the activities of certain overseas subsidiaries, the review of those operations being handled almost exclusively by another director.

Similar problems may occur at divisional and departmental level in a company. For example, a head of department may see himself as the driving force behind the business and start to behave more as owner than manager.

Mismatch between personality and status

In certain companies there may be a mismatch between the planned and actual power structure or hierarchy. Typically a forceful person in charge of a department or division exerts authority and influence disproportionate to his or her status. This may allow controls to be overridden or unfavourable information to be suppressed: conditions essential to the concealment of many frauds.

> ***Cooking the books***
>
> An aggressive manager in charge of a major development project ruled his department by fear. The project was delayed and required substantial extra resources. At his instigation reports to management outside the department were falsified by his staff to show a more favourable position.

Unusual behaviour

Anything surprising about the behaviour of individuals usually deserves further enquiry: for example a manager who keeps tedious responsibilities he would usually delegate, a supplier dealt with outside the purchasing system or abnormal levels of entertaining of one or two contacts, out of line with normal business practice.

> ***The self-sacrifice of our employees is touching . . .***
>
> A small overseas subsidiary always returned results exactly in line with its unchanging budget. During several years of high inflation none of the staff asked for or received any pay increases. In fact, the entire management and staff were colluding to steal all the profits in excess of the budget and had no need for pay increases.

Unusual business events or situations may also be warning signs of fraud. For example, unusual volumes of credit notes or bank reconciling items, accounting breakdowns or abrupt withdrawals of suppliers or customers. We look at some of these more detailed warning signs in relation to particular types of fraud in Chapters 4 and 5.

However, to detect the unusual it is important to define what the usual is. As the example opposite shows, this is not always easy.

Obsessive secrecy should be regarded with suspicion. A High Court judge once described secrecy as the 'badge of fraud'. Situations which may cause concern include:

> ***Shut door policy***
>
> Staff at a company became suspicious when the finance director was the only director/manager to start shutting his door. They became even more suspicious when he had his office soundproofed. He was later charged with fraud.

- information only provided when pressed for;
- the true nature of a transaction revealed only when it becomes clear that the questioner has most of the details; and
- transactions and structures which do not have a clear business purpose.

Fraudulent transactions often appear to have a valid business purpose. Fraudsters are expert at covering their tracks. Unusual behaviour may be the only clue that all is not well.

Illegal acts

Blatant acts of an illegal nature will inevitably cause concern. However, other apparently less serious breaches of legal or other internal requirements, or attitudes to such requirements, may be significant. For example, attitudes to Companies Act requirements regarding directors' interests or dealers' attitudes to position or counterparty limits may indicate something important about the culture of a company, its control environment or the integrity of individuals within it.

Expensive lifestyles

Lifestyles which are not commensurate with earnings are a well-known 'indicator of fraud'. For example, in one case a manager used to buy his staff champagne every Friday afternoon. In another, a manager used to change his Jaguar every year. His story was that his wife was extremely wealthy.

Although lifestyles of employees may not always be apparent, fraudsters are often unable to keep quiet about their new-found wealth. Never take the well-worn story about the inheritance at face value.

Certain companies make lifestyle checks on employees. Whether or not companies wish to do this is a matter of policy. However, whenever a company becomes aware of a significant mismatch between an employee's lifestyle and his earnings careful scrutiny of the transactions handled by the employee is advisable. Maintaining an expensive lifestyle may provide the motivation to commit further fraud.

Untaken holiday

Concealing fraud is not easy. Workaholics and staff who do not take their holidays may be trying to avoid the risk that their replacements might bring the fraud to light.

It is surprising how many frauds come to light when the fraudster is called away unavoidably. Enforcing holiday policy, a minimum of two clear weeks holiday for all staff, is crucial. However, ensuring proper cover during holiday absences is equally important.

Poor quality staff

A company can often be judged by its people. A company's inability to attract high calibre personnel usually indicates something about its reputation, its position in the marketplace, how it treats its staff or the culture of the company. Internal controls are only as effective as the people operating them.

Low morale

Low staff morale is conducive to fraud. Demotivated staff are less likely to operate controls effectively and may cut corners. In extreme circumstances, where a major redundancy programme is in progress or a site is to be closed, staff have been known to avenge themselves at the expense of the company by theft of assets or cash.

High staff turnover

> ***A dishonest manager***
>
> During an investigation staff who had recently resigned were interviewed. Several commented adversely on the character of their immediate manager: one stated that he was unwilling to work for a dishonest manager and provided evidence of specific frauds.

High staff turnover may indicate disquiet at fraudulent activity or the way the business is managed and a reluctance to continue working under such conditions.

Temporary staff should be used selectively and not entrusted with valuable assets. Companies should ensure that the screening procedures of recruitment agencies for temporary staff are consistent with their own.

Compensation tied to performance

Where remuneration is closely linked to financial performance it is important for checks to be made on the nature and quality of the profits generated by individuals remunerated on this basis.

Problems in this area have occurred in dealing rooms where high levels of bonus have been achieved by individual dealers based on the apparent profits which they have earned. Senior management may be reluctant to ask probing questions when dealers appear to be making a great deal of money for the company. However, unauthorised position taking, false deals or misuse of client accounts may underlie the apparent profits. An example of this problem in a dealing context is given under *Unrecorded deals* in the dealing section of Chapter 5.

Cultural risks

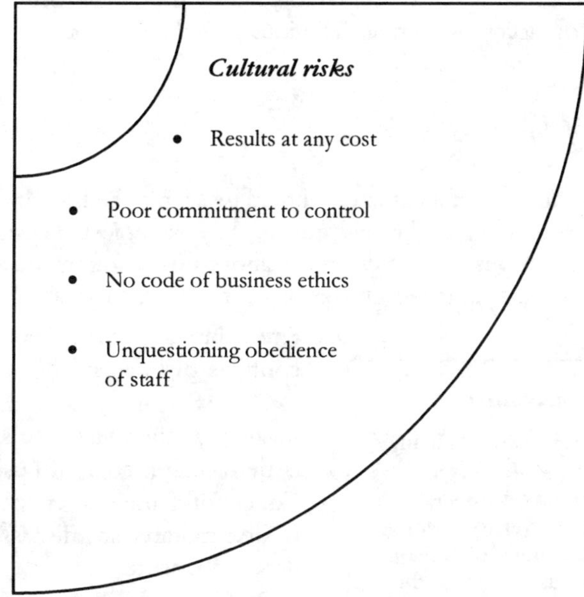

Results at any cost

Setting goals is an essential management tool but management may become so concerned with reaching financial or operational targets that this becomes the overriding aim at the expense of long term productivity or efficiency. In such cases management may be inclined to manipulate results to ensure achievement on paper.

Earnout schemes and bases of remuneration which are closely linked to performance (see above) may increase the risk of fraud.

Boosting an earnout

The managing director of a recently acquired business manipulated profits to increase payments to him under an earnout by paying certain expenses himself and overcharging customers.

Poor commitment to control

In certain companies there is general hostility to controls, regulation and audit. This may be due to a lack of commitment to these matters by directors or senior management. However, it may also be linked to other cultural factors such as too much emphasis on short term financial targets. Whatever the reason for hostility, these attitudes have a significant effect on the company's ability to protect itself against fraud.

Such attitudes may be demonstrated by attitudes to internal audit or inspection staff such as attempts to restrict the scope of the work and restrictions on access to certain individuals or documents.

No code of business ethics

The culture and tone of a company should be seen to be honest and opposed to fraud. Management at all levels must lead by example and ensure that rules are not bent, that business practices are above board and there are no hidden perks. It is essential to avoid grey areas in the rules, for example concerning entertainment, gifts, commissions or conflicts of interest.

Earned their dues

The manager of a company car scheme stole over 100 vehicles. Many were sold cheaply in secret to senior employees. None of these employees asked where the vehicles came from because they felt they had earned the bargains by hard work.

One way in which companies may make clear their views on such matters is by having a code of business ethics. Codes of business ethics and other related matters are discussed in more detail in Chapter 7.

Problems may occur in larger groups which have grown mainly through acquisitions. Variations in the business ethics may occur. For example, we know of one group in which there are three divisions each with a different code of business ethics and a fourth with no code at all.

A related problem is where groups of key staff in a business have worked together before in another company or country with poor ethics. The chances are that they will carry on in the same way. This may weaken the apparent segregation of duties or result in undue levels of trust being placed in particular individuals with inadequate review of their work.

Unquestioning obedience of staff

In certain cases staff may follow procedures by rote. This often occurs where there is an autocratic management style in a company or division. Sometimes this problem may occur where there are significant numbers of staff from overseas and there is a reluctance to return to a lower standard of living. In these circumstances staff may be more likely to acquiesce or collude in fraud or malpractice by their superiors. Scenarios include:

- staff are passive, showing no initiative;
- staff are in awe of their superiors;
- questioning of business decisions is not encouraged.

Structural risks

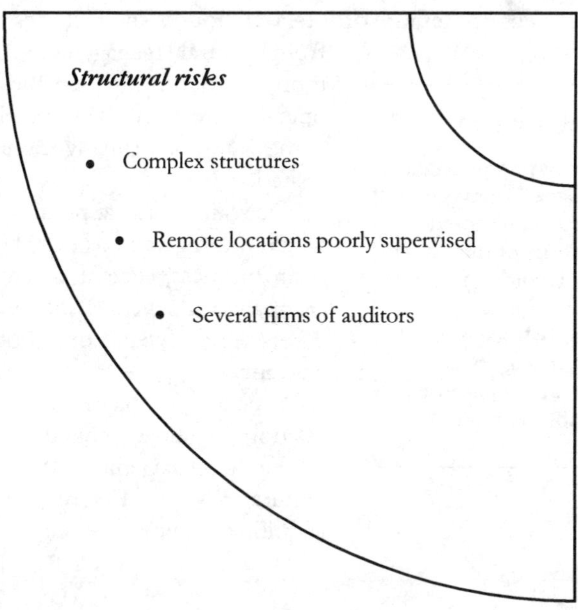

Complex structures

Many of the major reported frauds in recent years have involved the use of 'parallel' organisations – private companies under common ownership surrounding a 'public' or 'regulated' group. Typically a director or senior officer of the company, who is often also a significant shareholder, owns private companies which indirectly undertake transactions with the public or regulated group. The existence or ownership of the private companies is not disclosed.

A number of the frauds discussed in Chapters 4 and 5 of this guide use parallel organisations, for example for share support schemes, transactions in assets at other than market value or as devices to disguise the identity of a borrower, a customer or a supplier or to create circular refinancing arrangements.

Any suggestion of such structures should cause concern. Even where there are plausible explanations – for example tax reasons – this does not necessarily reduce the risk of fraud if the extent of such companies and their activities, and their relationship to the public or regulated group, is not fully understood by all the directors of a company and by all those who advise it.

Remote locations poorly supervised

Fraud is most likely to occur whenever management or supervision and control is least effective. Remote offices, warehouses and factories located far from central management may need more autonomy to enable them to operate effectively. This can be abused if they are not regularly monitored and visited.

The same risk applies to activities which are regarded as peripheral to the main business, such as management of company car schemes, disposal of fixed assets and repair of goods under warranty.

Particular problems may occur in relation to newly acquired subsidiaries where the management style or business culture may be different to that of the acquiring group.

> ***Black market sales***
>
> A remote and seldom visited subsidiary made black market sales to unlicensed customers. Some of the extra profits were recorded in the books to improve the margins. The balance was pocketed by managers and staff. Without the unlicensed trade, the subsidiary was unprofitable.

Several firms of auditors

The use of several firms of auditors within a group always increases risk and in certain circumstances may facilitate the concealment of fraud, especially where the auditors rarely communicate with each other. No one firm may have a proper understanding of the group's activities. Where there are a significant number of transactions between group companies and/or branches/divisions in different countries, fragmentation of the audit may be a particular problem.

The problem is compounded where there are parallel organisations (see above) audited by different auditors, with different year ends.

Business risks

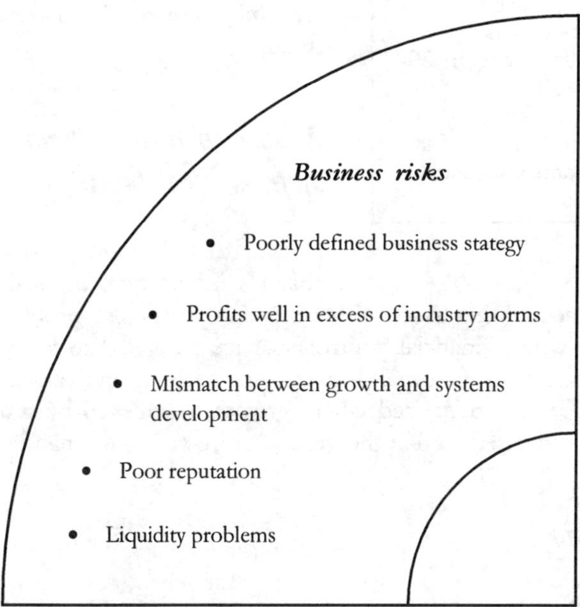

Poorly defined business strategy

Matters of corporate strategy and policy are crucial to developing a corporate culture which inhibits fraud. Poorly defined strategy, while not usually the direct cause of fraud, is often one of the key aspects which defines the environment in which fraud may thrive. Symptoms include low morale, high staff turnover and an inability to attract good staff or an undue emphasis on short-term targets. Corporate strategy is discussed further in Chapter 7.

Profits well in excess of industry norms

> ***Too good to be true***
>
> The vendor of an acquired business who remained with the company post-acquisition conspired with an employee of one of his major customers that they should accept invoices for 30 per cent more than were supplied. In return the vendor paid personally for home improvements at the employee's house, foreign holidays and other luxuries. The acquiring company became suspicious when the company achieved margins 20 per cent above any other in the industry and the amount due under the earnout clause of the acquisition contract appeared to be excessive.

Businesses which achieve results far in excess of industry norms should always be regarded with some suspicion; for example, rapid growth in sales, abnormal levels of profitability or an unusual ability to attract depositors or investors. These trends may indicate something about the nature of the product, the way it is sold, the customer base or the source of funds. Alternatively it may indicate that the company is overtrading and is heading for a liquidity crisis, which in turn may provide the motivation for fraud.

Mismatch between growth and systems development

Disparities between growth or changes in the type of business and the associated accounting systems have been a particular problem in the financial sector where financial controllers have struggled to keep up with rapid developments in financial instruments such as derivatives. Similar problems have been experienced where growth is achieved by acquisitions which are not assimilated so that the group outgrows its command structure.

Poor reputation

The views of other participants in the market are always important. Market reputation usually indicates something about the company's products, its people or its way of doing business. The characteristics identified by outsiders may highlight a factor which undermines the apparent defences of the company against fraud.

Liquidity problems

Tight liquidity may increase the motivation for fraud. A number of the examples considered in Chapters 4 and 5 were motivated by the need to meet regulatory limits or to give a more favourable impression of financial soundness.

Conclusion

In this chapter we have tried to draw together some of the factors which may increase the risk of fraud. As noted at the beginning of the chapter, no single factor on its own is likely to indicate fraud. However, where there is a combination of several factors there will usually be a high level of risk. This should lead to a rigorous examination of one or more aspects of the company's operations or individuals within it.

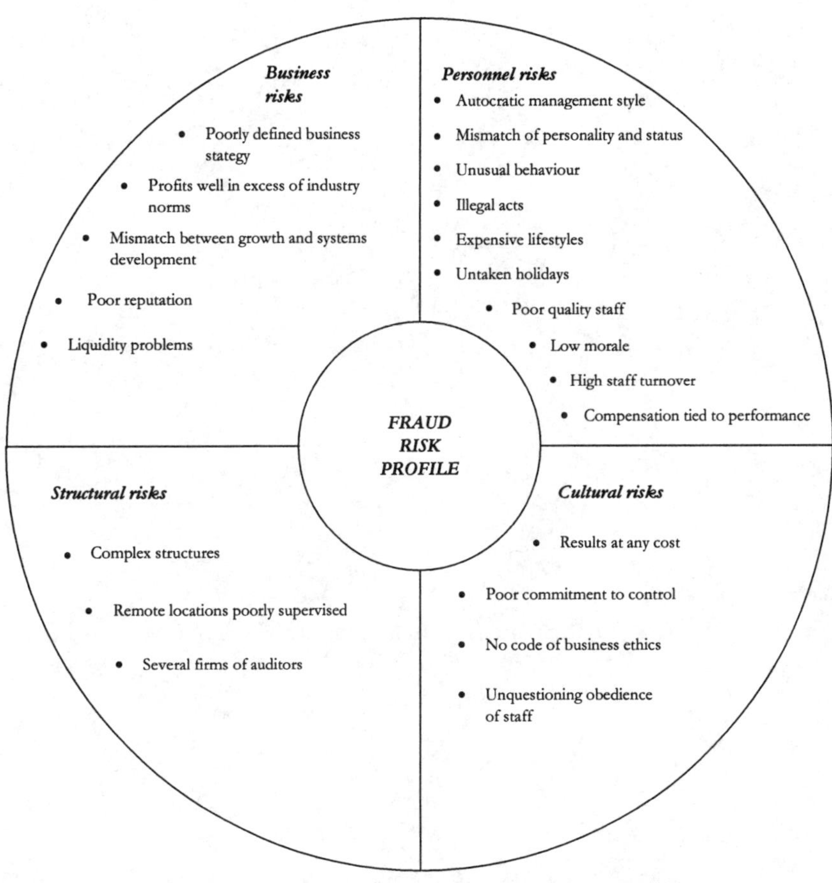

3 Knowing your enemy

Introduction

Fraudsters operate at different levels within and outside a company and in a wide variety of business circumstances. Each has his own motives and opportunities. In this chapter we identify briefly some of the common motives and attributes of fraudsters in actual cases. We do not attempt an in-depth psychological analysis of particular fraudsters.

Only a small proportion of frauds are planned in detail from the outset. People commit fraud when a motive coincides with an opportunity. The motive may be greed, lack of cash, revenge, a sense of ownership of the stolen property or of having earned it. The opportunity may arise because there is no real deterrent or little chance of discovery, or because there are grey areas in the rules. Over time the number of people who have the potential to commit fraud in a company is large. This makes it all the more important for companies to create an environment which inhibits fraud.

Motives

The range of possible motives is wide. Highlighted below are some of the motives underlying the examples of fraud included in this guide:

Motives

- Greed
- Financial problems
- Low loyalty
- Revenge
- Boredom

The above list is not intended to be comprehensive. Motives depend very much on particular circumstances.

Greed

Not surprisingly, greed is probably the most common motive. Fraudsters often 'slide down the slippery slope', starting with a falsified expense claim, then being tempted by a kickback from a vendor; they spend the proceeds, get a taste for the high life and then need to commit further fraud to maintain the lifestyle. Often staff do not realise what they are getting into.

However, other factors may provide the underlying motivation for greed, such as personal relationships. For example, a solicitor who defrauded 19 building societies of £4 million had two mistresses whom he flew around the world, spending hundreds of thousands of pounds on them. He had two houses in Florida, a villa in Spain and drove a Jaguar and a Cadillac. The fraud came to light when one mistress found out about the other.

Financial problems

A number of the frauds discussed later in this guide were motivated by the need to show a more favourable financial position or to meet regulatory requirements. The underlying problems may be increased competition and major changes in the cost structure leading to tight liquidity and an inability to meet key ratios in loan covenants.

> ***Under pressure to perform***
>
> The directors of a company which had recently been acquired, and on whom there was pressure to maintain profits, committed various frauds in collusion with suppliers. The directors arranged for a supplier to issue three credit notes amounting to £150,000 each to be offset against the cost of future purchases from that supplier.

We noted in the previous chapter that management may become so concerned with reaching financial or operational targets that this becomes an overriding aim. In such cases management may be inclined to manipulate results to ensure achievement on paper.

We also highlighted the risks involved when complex structures surround the group. If other companies owned by the fraudster are in financial difficulties he may find a way to draw on the funds of the main group to bail them out. This has occurred in a number of well known cases in recent years. It is surprising how often fraudsters see this type of fraud as 'borrowing'.

Low loyalty

Management and employees may feel they have not been suitably rewarded. For example, in one case certain Swiss banks paid commissions to another bank for the introduction of substantial client funds for discretionary management. The directors who had arranged the introductions believed that they personally, rather than the bank, should benefit from the commissions and with management collusion the commissions were paid on receipt to personal accounts of the directors.

When fraud is investigated it often turns out not to be an isolated occurrence. The fraudster may have committed other frauds, or other staff in the organisation may have committed fraud. If the motivation is there, then the temptation to commit fraud may be increased where a member of staff sees others, in particular more senior staff, 'getting away with it'.

Revenge

Revenge is sometimes a factor in certain types of fraud. It may be due to perceived exploitation of employees, frustrated ambition, demotion of certain individuals following a reorganisation or takeover or low morale due to a redundancy programme.

Boredom

In certain types of technically complex frauds boredom may be a factor. The computer technician who feels frustrated in his job may try to find ways to 'beat the system'. The initial motivation may not be fraud but more in the nature of 'personal achievement'. This type of motivation is not as common as may be thought. However, it is a factor to be considered where there are relatively junior staff with very high levels of technical expertise compared to their managers.

Attributes

Fraudsters use a wide range of techniques, the common aim being to conceal the fraud through deception. The following character sketches serve to illustrate some of the more common aspects of deceptive behaviour. None of these aspects in themselves indicates fraud. They may however be the first clue that all is not well.

1 Successful Sam

- Boasts about having all the right contacts
- Talks over-optimistically about business prospects
- Gives the impression of being wealthy and successful
- Entertains or is entertained lavishly
- Flatters people to make them feel important

2 Eva the deceiver

- Does not allow anyone to see the full picture
- Says as little as possible unless confronted with the facts
- Answers different questions from the ones put
- Uses delaying tactics – always about to go to an important meeting
- Passes the parcel
- Goes on the attack when questioned closely about matters she would prefer not to disucss

3 Martin the manipulator

- Has his door closed rather a lot of the time
- Manipulates timetables and deadlines
- Exploits ignorance – blinds people with science
- Carefully controls access to certain personnel, customers or suppliers
- Deals with certain accounts personally outside the main system
- Plays off various advisers against each other

4 Conscientious Connie

- Never takes a holiday
- Seemingly very conscientious
- Keeps people off her patch
- If absent unavoidably, ensures that all problems are left for her return
- Loner/alien

The key point is to focus on behavioural issues. How people respond to questions is often as important as what is actually said. It is easier to conceal than to falsify. It is easier for the fraudster to say nothing (because the right questions are not asked) than maintain 'a story' under close questioning.

4 FRAUD IN MANUFACTURING AND SERVICES

Introduction

In this chapter we look at the key risks facing companies in the manufacturing and services sectors. The main business cycles are examined in turn – sales, purchases, inventory and cash and payment systems. We identify the points in each cycle at which the risk of fraud is greatest. Frauds in other areas are also discussed, such as irregular dealings in a company's shares, the misuse of government funding and the misuse of assets under the company's control. We identify the common warning signs for each type of fraud. We conclude by highlighting a number of frauds which are particularly prevalent in the public sector.

The indicators of fraud discussed in Chapter 2 should be considered alongside the guidance given in this chapter. For example, lifestyles not commensurate with earnings or employees not taking holiday may be indicators that all is not well in a wide range of situations. Similarly, employee groupings may undermine the apparent segregation of duties, for example where employees have worked together before at a previous employer, and other behavioural and cultural factors may be significant issues.

Investigations often find that there is a number of interconnected frauds, spanning various operational areas. Most of the major reported cases have involved combinations of several different types of fraud or the same fraud committed on a number of occasions. In this chapter we discuss each type of fraud separately so that the various risks and the warning signs may be seen more clearly.

Sales

There are four key phases in a typical sales cycle:

- receipt of the sales order;
- delivery of the goods or services;
- invoicing and recording of the sale; and
- collection of the cash or dealing with the bad debt.

In practice there are many more detailed processing steps but for the purposes of this chapter it is helpful to keep these four key phases clearly in mind.

In the first phase the main concerns are whether the company receives all the sales orders it should (i.e. they are not diverted) and whether its customers are genuine and do not misrepresent their identity or credit status. Management and employee frauds in this phase include diversion of sales and the use of bogus intermediary companies to manipulate margins and 'cream off' profits. External frauds include the use of false names and addresses by customers, the misrepresentation of credit status or what is known as 'long firm' fraud (this term is explained below).

In the second phase of the cycle, the delivery of the goods or services, the key concern is whether the customer receives the product or service which he ordered. The major fraud in this phase of the cycle is the supply of non-existent or substandard goods or services or short deliveries. External frauds include counterfeiting of branded products.

In the third phase of the cycle, invoicing and recording the sale, the key concern is whether the goods and services are properly invoiced and that the invoices represent actual sales. Management and employee frauds in this phase include fictitious sales, kickbacks to or from customers, underbilling or underringing (i.e., of tills) and pre-invoicing.

In the final phase of the cycle, collection of the cash, the main concern is whether cash is collected in respect of all sales and whether cash is deposited and recorded promptly. Typical management and employee frauds include 'teeming and lading', sometimes referred to as 'lapping' fraud, and writing off receivables for a fee. There is also a number of frauds which relate more specifically to the cash area itself. We deal with these later in the chapter under *Cash and payment systems.*

The above frauds are illustrated in the following chart:

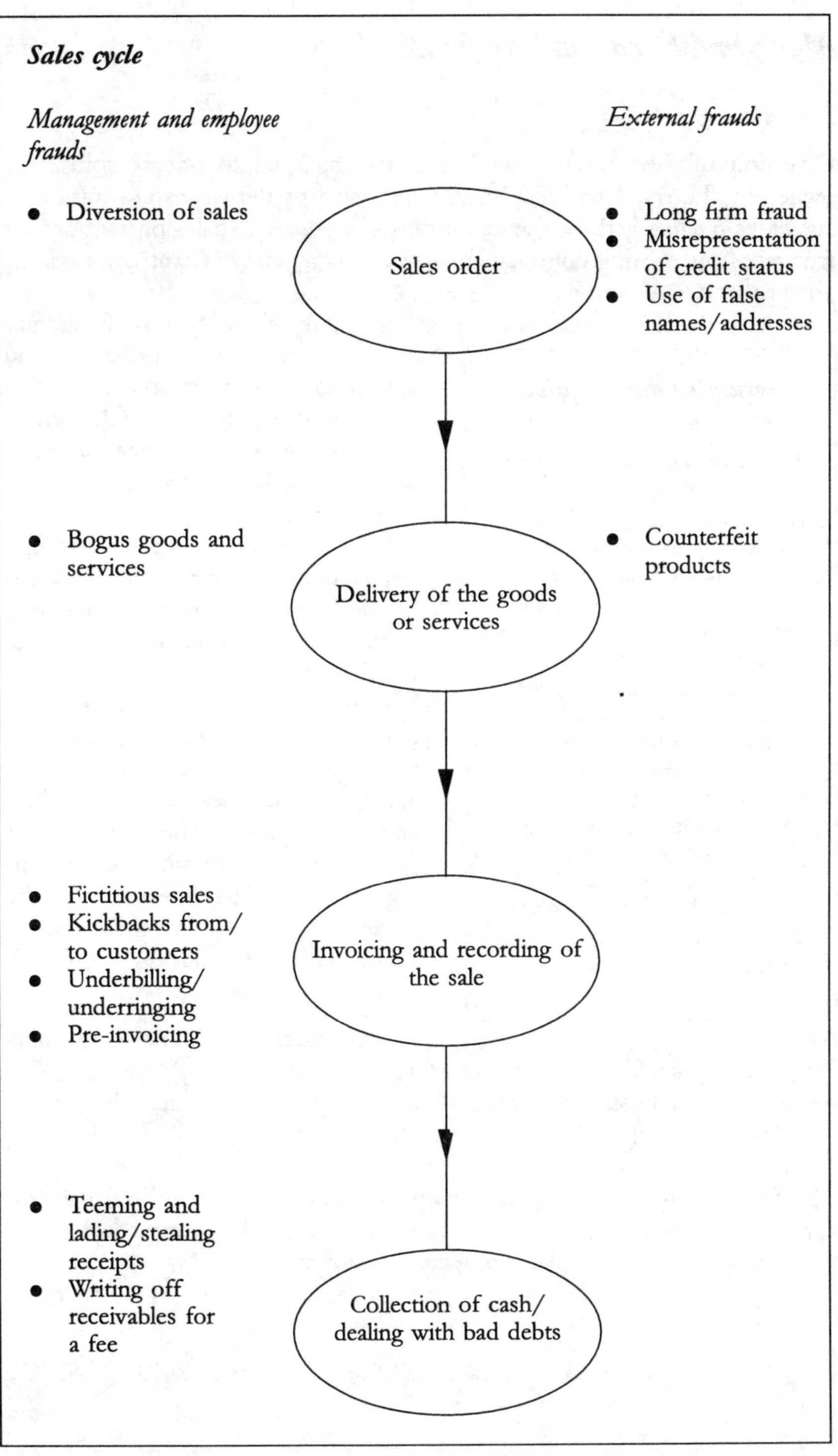
Sales cycle
Management and employee frauds
External frauds
Diversion of sales
Sales order
Long firm fraud
Misrepresentation of credit status
Use of false names/addresses
Bogus goods and services
Delivery of the goods or services
Counterfeit products
Fictitious sales
Kickbacks from/ to customers
Underbilling/ underringing
Pre-invoicing
Invoicing and recording of the sale
Teeming and lading/stealing receipts
Writing off receivables for a fee
Collection of cash/ dealing with bad debts

Management and employee frauds

Diversion of sales

Diversion of sales usually involves re-routing sales to private companies owned by the fraudster. This may be achieved by the fraudster's misuse of customer mailing lists, or the diversion of responses to sales promotions, or frustration of existing contracts, by using uncompetitive terms or providing poor service.

The risk of this type of fraud may be particularly high prior to and following an acquisition or major reorganisation, for example where the vendors remain in the business, where staff have been demoted or where morale is low.

Sales may also be routed through bogus intermediary companies owned by the fraudster or his associates (e.g., brokers or distributors) with the fraudster taking a cut in the form of hidden commissions or unusual pricing structures. For example, an intermediary used by a company for exports overcharged for import dues and taxes, passing over the correct amounts to the authorities and retaining the rest. The intermediary was owned by the sales director's wife.

Warning signs include:

- unexpected loss of customers or a high level of customer complaints (assuming such complaints are monitored independently); and
- inconsistent business patterns – for example, sales reduced but spares sales constant (or vice versa).

The risk of this type of fraud is increased where there is no independent appraisal of pricing structures or amounts charged by intermediaries and where ownership of supplier companies is not checked.

> ***Disgruntled director diverts sales***
>
> The ex-director of a company, which had recently been acquired and divisionalised, and who remained with the group, diverted sales to a rival company owned by him. He ensured his employer's tenders for contracts were uncompetitive and that poor service was given on other contracts. He recommended the rival company as an alternative to perform the contracts. Management of the parent company realised something was wrong when several staff left the division and the division was underperforming against budget.

Bogus goods and services

Bogus product frauds have been particularly prevalent in the financial sector in recent years, with fake financial products being sold to unsuspecting private investors. These frauds are discussed in the next chapter.

New ventures involving management or staff without a proven track record are a higher risk. The nature of the customer base is also important. Relevant factors include the vulnerability of the customers and their ability to appraise the product or service.

More generally these frauds involve management and employees manipulating a particular product or service in order to meet profit targets or to siphon off part of the product for personal benefit. This type of fraud involves the provision of sub-standard or non-existent products or services to customers. Examples are clocked cars in the motor trade or sale of watered down spirits in public houses or hotels.

> ***The holiday homes that never got off the ground***
>
> A company allegedly sold thousands of pounds worth of timeshares on properties abroad. It was alleged that no building work was ever undertaken and the scheme would not have obtained planning permission. The pictures in the brochure were of another development.

Warning signs include:

- products which are 'too good to be true' – for example, low risk, high return products;
- grandiose claims and glossy advertising which cannot be easily corroborated;
- services provided at remote locations or at a date far in the future (particularly where up-front payments or deposits are required);
- explanation of transaction is complex, with exotic reasons for advantageous pricing; and
- abnormal growth or profitability.

Fictitious sales

Fictitious sales frauds involve the generation of false invoices or the manipulation of prices or quantities to increase turnover. This may involve:

- issuing dummy invoices to fictitious customers;
- making sales to 'friendly customers', with an undisclosed agreement to buy back the goods at a later date;
- overcharging customers; or
- kickbacks to customer staff to accept higher prices/quantities.

For example, in one case a company issued dummy invoices for stock which

> ***Boosting an earnout***
>
> The managing director of a recently acquired business manipulated profits to increase payments to him under an earnout by overcharging customers and paying certain expenses himself.

was old, on sale or return or on display and the profit recognised although no payment was expected. Old invoices were redated so that they would appear as current on the aged debt report. In another case a company agreed to 'sell' goods to one of its distributors with an agreement to buy back the goods after the year end at a higher price.

The motivation for such frauds will be higher when market conditions are difficult. Excessive pressure on management to meet financial targets or tight liquidity may also increase risk, for example, where loan covenants may be breached if key ratios are not met.

Warning signs include:

- unusual fluctuations in sales especially around the year end;
- an unusual number of journals, credit notes or other adjustments, especially in months following the audit visit;
- circularisations refused for particular customers;
- customers dealt with outside the normal system (for example, handled exclusively by a senior member of staff using non-standard documentation);
- evasive answers concerning movements on particular accounts;
- inconsistent changes in activity levels – for example, high sales in period but no change in distribution costs; and
- changes in business patterns – for example, entry into new, remote markets.

Kickbacks to/from customers

Kickbacks to or from customers involve the payment of a kickback of some kind in return for manipulating quantities or prices or supplying a higher grade of product. The risk of this type of fraud is increased where there is no independent review of prices and/or terms of business for particular customers. Kickbacks may also be paid to employees to write off debts or issue credit notes. This is discussed in more detail below.

> ***Splitting the difference***
>
> A sales director agreed a reduced price for a particular customer. In fact, the arrangement was that the customer would receive half the agreed reduction, the remainder being paid to the sales director personally.

A further example of this type of fraud was referred to in Chapter 2 under *Business risks.*

Warning signs include:

- customers dealt with outside the main system, for example, handled exclusively by a senior member of staff using non-standard documentation;
- no pricing information on standing data or unusual prices, discounts or terms, or extent of credit given;
- unusual trends in margins; and
- alterations on invoices or other documentation.

Underbilling/underringing

Underbilling involves the suppression of invoices, the understating of quantities despatched or the manipulation of prices or discounts, often in return for some kind of kickback to the employee. Underringing is the underrecording of cash sales, for example shop employees not ringing up sales in retail outlets and pocketing the amount not recorded.

Warning signs include:

- alterations to delivery notes or invoices;
- transactions handled exclusively by a senior member of staff using non-standard documentation; and
- certain customers dealt with by only one member of staff.

The risk of this type of fraud is increased where there is:

- no sequential control over invoices;
- no independent checks on prices;
- weak controls over changes to standing data or the absence of standing data for particular customers;
- poor control over 'miscellaneous' sales;
- poor control over till rolls; and
- no reconciliation of stock movements to sales.

Pre-invoicing

> **_Papering over the cracks_**
>
> The general manager of a company pre-invoiced sales to hide very poor trading results. He also made insufficient provision for slow-moving stock, representing that orders were in hand for particular stock lines.

Pre-invoicing involves bringing forward the date of sale or the apparent completion of longer-term contracts artificially with a view to inflating turnover. For example, in one case a completion certificate was wrongly obtained in return for an undisclosed side letter to the contract customer confirming that certain outstanding contractual obligations would be performed (see *Omitted contingencies* below).

As with *Fictitious sales*, the motivation for this type of fraud will be higher when market conditions are difficult, when there is excessive pressure on management to meet financial targets or when liquidity is tight. Warning signs are as for *Fictitious sales* above.

Teeming and lading/stealing receipts

Perhaps the best known fraud in the sales area is 'teeming and lading'. This involves the theft of cash or cheque receipts on a sales ledger and the use of later receipts, or receipts from other customers, to 'settle' the outstanding amounts. The fraudster conceals the unpaid amounts for as long as possible until he is able to repay the amount or, more likely, until he disappears.

Teeming and lading frauds are rarely reported in the press. This is because they do not usually involve significant amounts and tend to be committed by more junior staff. However, quite often other frauds may be linked to teeming and lading so this should not give any particular comfort.

Poor segregation of duties, not only between the recording of sales and the handling of cash and cheques but also between these functions and the resolution of customer complaints, increases the risk of teeming and lading significantly.

Warning signs include:

- part-paid items on the sales ledger;
- large numbers of journals or adjustments on particular accounts or on bank reconciliations;
- unusual fluctuations or inconsistencies on the aged debtor analysis;
- alterations to invoices or frequent issue of 'duplicates' on particular accounts;
- differences between original and duplicate paying-in slips or incomplete details or alterations; and
- differences between paying-in slips, cash book details and ledger

A 'computer error'

A sales ledger clerk stole a number of cheques. He told the customers to ignore the outstanding items on their statements, saying it was a 'computer error'. Eventually he had to make a significant transfer from another account, at which point the fraud was discovered.

A creative accountant

A temporary accountant, who was responsible for credit control, stole cheques payable to his employer. He opened two bank accounts in the name of the company. He paid them into the new accounts. The fraud was concealed for a time by bogus journal entries and teeming and lading of sales ledger accounts.

postings – for example, regarding the number of items, dates and payee details.

The risk of this type of fraud is increased where there is:

- no independent review of customers who do not pay or who delay payment; and
- no independent despatch of statements or investigation of complaints or queries.

Writing off receivables for a fee

As already noted, customers may pay kickbacks to staff in a variety of situations. In the collection phase, credit controllers or other staff may be bribed by a customer to write off outstanding debts and to frustrate legal action, for example, by introducing aspects which may make pursuit of an action more difficult. A possible warning sign of this type of fraud is heavy concentration of provisions/write-offs attributable to one employee or division.

External frauds

Long firm fraud

In long firm fraud the fraudster obtains goods on credit, purporting to be running a bona fide business. Initially orders are small and payments are made promptly. As the supplier's confidence increases so does the size of the orders and further credit is given. After a few months, when the fraudster believes he has obtained the maximum credit he can obtain, he disposes of the goods quickly at discount prices for cash and disappears without trace, leaving the supplier bills unpaid.

> ***Here today, gone tomorrow***
>
> A fraudster set up an electrical retail business. Initially he paid supplier bills promptly. Then he placed larger orders and obtained increased credit. After a few months, he quickly sold off his stock at discount prices and disappeared, leaving the supplier bills unpaid.

Long firm fraud is probably one of the oldest white-collar crimes. The Victorians complained of the fraudulent activities of 'phantom capitalists'. More recently during the recession with companies desperate for sales, long firm fraud has been prevalent. Quite often long firm fraudsters, if caught, produce convincing alibis, including burglary, flood or fire.

Long firm fraud tends to be carried out on a highly organised basis by gangs of fraudsters operating a number of linked businesses using false identities. The risk of long firm fraud is greatly increased where customers are situated in remote locations, making face-to-face contact unlikely.

Warning signs include:

- an air of unreality about the principals or their business premises, for example lack of customer orientation;
- rapidly increasing turnover for new customers; and
- no independent checks on the existence or credentials of referees.

Misrepresentation of credit status/use of false names and addresses

This type of fraud includes a wide range of practices which involve impersonation or the submission of false or misleading information.

Warning signs include:

- poor quality documentation;
- use of 'accommodation' offices by new customers;
- customers who operate through 'front' companies or intermediaries; and
- incomplete customer details or undue difficulties in completing normal credit references and other checks.

Counterfeit products

Counterfeiting of branded goods is a widespread problem. Most companies are alert to the risks in this area. Detailed consideration of this type of fraud is outside the scope of this guide.

Purchases

We now look at the main risks in the purchases cycle. Once again it is helpful to focus on the main phases in the business cycle and the risks which need to be managed at each stage. As with the sales cycle, there are four main phases:

- selection of the supplier and ordering the goods or services;
- receipt of the goods or services;
- receipt and recording of the supplier invoice; and
- payment of the invoice.

In the first phase the key concerns are that there should be a truly competitive bidding process and that only properly authorised orders are processed. Typical management and employee frauds in this phase include the release of confidential information by employees of the purchasing company to particular suppliers to favour their bids usually in return for some kind of kickback. External frauds include bid rigging and advance fee fraud, whereby companies are persuaded to part with an up-front fee or deposit with the promise of future delivery, the fraudster then disappearing without trace.

In the second phase of the cycle, the receipt of the goods or services, the main concern is that goods or services of the correct quantity and quality are supplied. Management and employee frauds include work to be done or goods supplied for private purposes (so the goods are never delivered to the company at all). External frauds include short deliveries and the supply of sub-standard products.

In the third phase of the cycle, receipt and recording of the supplier's invoice, the first concern is whether the supplier invoice is genuine. The second concern is whether the prices and quantities on the invoice are correct. Typical management and employee frauds include the creation of dummy suppliers, the use of connected companies or bogus intermediary companies, and the misuse of credit notes, rebates and volume discounts. External frauds include billing for work not performed and overbilling.

In the final phase of the cycle, payment of the invoice, the main concern is that payments are only made in respect of authorised invoices and that proper security is maintained over cheque books and the use of money transfer systems. Frauds in this phase of the cycle are discussed under *Cash and payment systems* below.

The above frauds are illustrated in the chart overleaf:

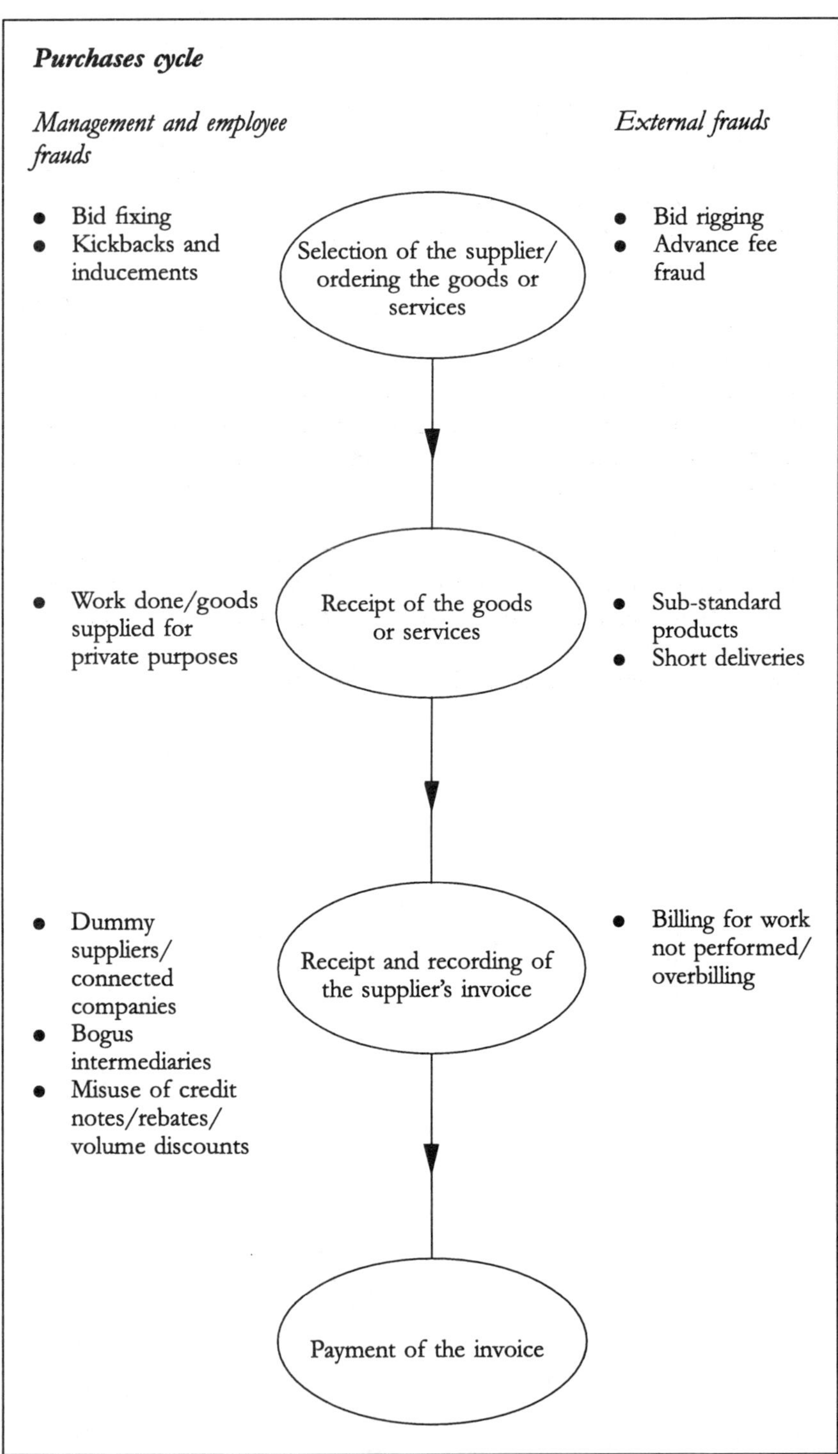
Purchases cycle
Management and employee frauds
External frauds
Bid fixing
Kickbacks and inducements
Selection of the supplier/ ordering the goods or services
Bid rigging
Advance fee fraud
Work done/goods supplied for private purposes
Receipt of the goods or services
Sub-standard products
Short deliveries
Dummy suppliers/ connected companies
Bogus intermediaries
Misuse of credit notes/rebates/ volume discounts
Receipt and recording of the supplier's invoice
Billing for work not performed/ overbilling
Payment of the invoice

Management and employee frauds

Bid fixing

In bid fixing, bidders obtain inside information, usually in return for a kickback paid to an employee of the purchasing company. The information may relate to the selection criteria, technical specifications or the prices of other bids. The effect of bid fixing is that the purchasing company obtains less favourable terms and pays a higher price than it would otherwise have done had a truly competitive process been in operation. However, in certain cases the effect is much more damaging. The specifications for an entire project may be inappropriate.

> ***Information brokers***
>
> Employees in a major civil engineering company passed inside information to 'information brokers' who in turn passed it to one of the bidders for a large contract. The information related to the selection criteria being used by the purchasing company and the prices of other bids. The information enabled the supplier to pitch its bid 10 per cent (£20 million) higher than the price it would otherwise have submitted.

In large manufacturing or contracting companies this type of fraud can be a significant problem. So-called 'information brokers' may act as intermediaries between employees of the purchasing company who divulge the confidential information and tendering companies who wish to buy such information so that they may obtain lucrative contracts. The brokers make it more difficult to trace the source of the leak. Payments of kickbacks may also be concealed by the brokers, using front companies in offshore locations and/or numbered bank accounts in countries with strict bank secrecy laws.

Warning signs include:

- abnormal prices or terms (specifications which can only be met by one supplier);
- prices of bids close together;
- well-known suppliers not asked to tender;
- pre-qualified suppliers;
- small supplier/large contract; supplier small relative to size of purchasing company;
- location of supplier unusual: for example remote supplier used for routine services or supplier providing services outside normal range of business;
- tenders accepted after closing date;
- high level of extras/claims by particular suppliers;

- changes to the specifications or price soon after the contract is awarded; and
- a large number of invoices for particular supplier just beneath approval threshold, thereby avoiding more formal tendering procedures.

Other clues are the use of particular brokers or consultants in the bid process, common names, addresses or solicitors between various bidders, waivers of normal business terms and conditions and procurement staff being unduly defensive when questioned about particular contracts. Other relevant matters include whether or not vendor complaints are handled independently and whether former suppliers or unsuccessful bidders are debriefed.

Kickbacks and inducements

Kickbacks and inducements may be used in a wide range of purchasing frauds to induce employees to favour particular suppliers. The frauds discussed above relate to the more formal tendering procedures used in connection with the award of major contracts. However, similar practices may be used in virtually any business in relation to other contracts, for example relating to the installation of computer equipment, office refurbishment, maintenance, design and consultancy contracts. Many large companies which own major brands incur significant advertising, marketing and promotion expenditure. Kickbacks and other arrangements involving conflicts of interest are common in this area.

> ***A luxury car and £20,000 in cash***
>
> The director of a company allegedly accepted a luxury car and £20,000 in cash to favour a particular builder which had tendered for refurbishment work at its offices.

Kickbacks are difficult to detect because there may be no obvious clue that a kickback has been given in the books of the purchasing company. The evidence, if any, will usually be in the records of the supplying company. For that reason certain companies incorporate provisions for vendor audits in their contracts with suppliers to monitor key accounts such as entertaining and related expenditure. The incidence of kickbacks and inducements is likely to be higher where a company does not have a clear policy concerning the acceptance of gifts, bribes and inducements.

Warning signs are as for *Bid fixing* above.

Work done/goods supplied for private purposes

In the second phase of the purchases cycle, the receipt of the goods or services, one of the most common frauds is the obtaining of goods or

Keeping the house up to scratch

Staff in a maintenance department incorporated into their schedule work on their own homes. They removed the necessary supplies from inventory and falsified their time records (even charging overtime for the private work).

services for private purposes. This may involve the fraudster appropriating company assets or using company time for private purposes. The risk of this type of fraud is increased where activities are conducted at remote locations or are not closely supervised.

Warning signs include:

- unusual delivery times or methods;
- ambiguous or abbreviated descriptions on invoices; and
- over-ordered or surplus stock lines.

The risk of this type of fraud is increased where there is:

- a weak link between invoices and the origination of the order; and
- poor segregation of duties.

Dummy suppliers and connected companies

Companies may have strong controls over the initial selection of suppliers in relation to major contracts but may monitor the later submission of invoices under the contract less well, when inflated or false invoices may be introduced. Controls may also be weaker in relation to certain contracts, for example, relating to computer installations, office refurbishments, maintenance, design and other consultancy work. Although these are probably the areas of highest risk, dummy suppliers and connected companies can feature in virtually any area of a company's purchasing activity.

A phantom transport company

A road haulage manager set up a bogus transport company and over eight months invoiced his employer £150,000. He bought luxury cars, foreign holidays and luxurious fittings for his home. He had so many cars he was able to set up a car hire business.

Payments may be made to dummy suppliers for services never provided or amounts posted to accounts of suppliers which the company has in fact stopped using. Amounts may be posted to accounts which are 'off budget' (such as recharge accounts) or 'up-front' payments or deposits may be made in respect of bogus contracts. Another fraud in this area is 'teeming and lading' with suppliers. The fraudster changes the payee detail on a cheque, or sets up a bank account in a supplier's name, diverts the cheque to the account and uses later cheques made payable to the supplier to 'settle' the earlier unpaid liability.

Warning signs include:

- unclear reasons for particular supplies or few details concerning the service provided;
- suppliers not generally known to staff, not handled in the normal way, or dealt with exclusively by a director or manager;
- suppliers with PO Box addresses, accommodation addresses, residential addresses, the same address as another supplier, as an employee or his next of kin or an employee's former employer;
- invoices which are soiled, incomplete, over-abbreviated or altered in some way;
- unfolded invoices (that have never been in the mail);
- invoices from various suppliers on similar stationery;
- corporate suppliers with no registered number, using accommodation address or resident offshore;
- supplier has incorrect value added tax number;
- large number of invoices for a particular supplier just beneath approval thresholds;
- numerous contras or other adjustments on purchase ledger;
- numerous entries in suspense accounts during the year;
- confirmation of supplier accounts resisted or unusual conditions suggested; and
- supplier does not offer usual discounts and special deals.

Bogus consultancy and design services

The finance director of an information systems company defrauded the company of £1.5 million over a five year period. For instance he paid £275,000 for computer consultancy never received. He also paid £348,000 to an interior design company in Florida, falsely claiming that the company had provided services to his employer. In fact the sums were channelled back to him and were used to buy three properties in Florida. He also bought computer hardware and then resold it privately or sometimes gave it away.

The risk of this type of fraud is increased where:

- there are weak account opening procedures or weak controls over amendments to standing data;
- there is poor control over dormant supplier accounts;
- there is poor control over paid invoices; and
- there are no zero-based budgets or clearly defined budget holders for particular accounts.

Bogus intermediaries

Prices or quantities may be manipulated or products substituted by bogus intermediaries. This is most likely to happen where the intermediary is acting for an overseas supplier with whom it is difficult for the purchasing company to have direct contact. Unnecessary or exorbitant charges may be built into the price charged to the purchasing company.

Warning signs include:

- ownership or status of intermediaries not known;
- reason for intermediary arrangements not clear; and
- vendor complaints not monitored independently.

Misuse of credit notes, rebates and volume discounts

The true cost of purchases may be manipulated through the misuse of credit notes or volume discounts and rebates. For example, credit notes may be used to manipulate profits or to conceal other frauds. Alternatively volume discounts and rebates may be triggered artificially and diverted for the personal benefit of the fraudster.

Warning signs include:

- abnormal numbers and/or value of credit notes around period ends;
- volume discounts/rebates not monitored independently against quantities bought; and
- stock surpluses (indicating possible overpurchasing) to trigger volume discounts.

> ***A rebate disguised as a loan repayment***
>
> A supplier sent a cheque for a volume rebate to the managing director of a company. He paid it into one of the company's dormant bank accounts personally and issued instructions to the bank to transfer the funds to the company's normal trading account. He told the company's accountant that this was some of his own money which should be credited to his personal account. The money was subsequently withdrawn by the director.

External frauds

Bid rigging

Bid rigging is the manipulation of the competitive bidding process. Typically, bidders conspire to agree among themselves the prices and terms for particular contracts. Contracts are then allocated between the conspirators in rotation. As with bid fixing, the effect is that the purchasing company obtains less favourable terms and pays a higher price than it would otherwise have done had a truly competitive process been in operation.

Warning signs are as for *Bid fixing* above.

Advance fee fraud

Advance fee fraud has attracted a good deal of publicity in recent years. Typically the fraudster takes an up-front fee or deposit and promises to deliver certain goods or services in the future. However, once he has pocketed the fee (or several fees) he disappears.

> **_Cheap Ferraris_**
>
> A car dealer took £3.5 million in deposits from 1,100 motorists promising that he would obtain Rolls Royces, Ferraris, Aston Martins and Porches at very low prices. He rarely delivered the cars.

Those most at risk are businessmen who are having difficulty in obtaining a particular product or service (for example, access to credit). The fraudster exploits this vulnerability. Others may be tempted by unusually low prices offered by the fraudster.

Warning signs include:

- abnormally low prices or products or services which seem 'too good to be true';
- non-returnable up-front payments or deposits required;
- all dealings through agents;
- inability to verify the authenticity of documentation;
- all correspondence and documentation is faxed;
- complex explanations given for advantageous terms or reasons for undisclosed principal entering into deal;
- deal involves complex and unusual financial instruments;
- purported principal is overseas and identity cannot be revealed; and
- the agent is in a hurry to conclude the deal.

The transactions often involve foreign agents who claim they are acting for foreign government departments or for foreign leaders 'who must remain anonymous'.

Short deliveries/goods not supplied

Short deliveries and invoicing for goods not supplied is a common problem. Companies at greatest risk are those with:

- weak controls over goods received;
- poor physical security;
- weak account opening procedures; or

> ***Taking a slice***
>
> A canteen manager, who worked for a catering company, colluded with the van driver of the food supplier to the client company to invoice larger quantitites than had been delivered. The surplus was sold and the proceeds split between the canteen manager and the van driver.

- a weak link between the origination of the order, receipt of the goods and approval of the invoice.

Warning signs include:

- stock shortages;
- deliveries at unusual times or at unusual locations; and
- tampering with measuring equipment.

Sub-standard products

Sub-standard product frauds can be devastating where the products supplied are for use in sophisticated equipment. Those most at risk from this type of fraud are companies which do not have rigorous quality control checks on goods supplied or no independent checks on the credentials or capabilities of key suppliers.

Sometimes grandiose claims are made by suppliers about work they have performed for other customers, for example major public companies, overseas governments and members of royal families. It is surprising how often such claims are accepted at face value without any further corroboration.

High risk situations are where suppliers are changed at the last moment, where there are rushed jobs, or where the terms require substantial payment in advance of delivery.

> ***'Bought in Hong Kong'***
>
> An electronics engineer was sub-contracted by an approved supplier of a major organisation to supply military-grade adjustable voltage regulators for use in submarine torpedoes. In fact he supplied parts which he obtained from a shop in Hong Kong. He produced false certificates supposedly issued by the company which normally supplied the regulators. He told the approved supplier that he had managed to obtain war stock parts from the United States and from the grounded space shuttle programme.

Billing for work not performed/overbilling

This type of fraud is similar to *Short deliveries/goods not supplied* above. Susceptible contracts are those where a large number of invoices is submitted, the service is supplied at a remote location or checking performance of individual stages of the contract is difficult.

As with most purchasing frauds a clear link between payment of the invoice and the need for the supply is fundamental to prevention.

> ***Little and often***
>
> Under a contract to service a road fleet of 7,000 vehicles, a supplier was not allowed to make a profit on parts supplied. To compensate for this restriction the supplier allegedly added an amount to each invoice. Although the amount added to each invoice was small, the total loss was very considerable.

Warning signs include:

- no independent checks on prices or volume discounts;
- no competitive tendering;
- no zero-based budgeting; and
- vague terms in contracts and no detailed review of charges such as travel, advertising, consultancy fees, recruitment, maintenance, and leasing.

Inventory

We have discussed above a number of frauds which concern the receipt or despatch of goods. However, a number of frauds relate specifically to the holding of inventory. The key concern is theft of inventory. However, there are a number of other related frauds in this area including theft of returned stock or valuable scrap and the misuse of metering and weighbridge equipment.

Inventory records may also be manipulated to conceal frauds in other areas.

> ***Inventory frauds***
>
> - Theft of inventory
> - Theft of returned stock
> - Theft of valuable scrap
> - Metering and weighbridge frauds
> - Manipulation of inventory records

Management and employee frauds

Theft of inventory

Inventory fraud is endemic in certain industries. The frauds are often conducted on a highly organised basis and involve a large number of employees, sometimes acting in collusion with organised criminals. The frauds may remain undetected for many years. Businesses handling valuable and easily moveable products (such as electrical goods and motor vehicle spare parts) are especially vulnerable.

For example, four employees at an electrical goods manufacturer stole spare parts over an eight-year period. The fraud was masterminded by an electrical salesman, assisted by a lorry driver and forklift driver. The salesman's uncle delivered the stolen parts to shops around the country. The spare parts were sold at a discount.

Certain inventory frauds occur either on the delivery route from the supplier or on the delivery route to the customer. For example, in one case delivery drivers en route from a manufacturing plant to a distribution warehouse would unload a portion of the load at another warehouse. The delivery driver then colluded with the goods-in clerk at the distribution warehouse to sign off the goods received note for the quantity stated on the delivery note whereas the amount actually delivered was less. The delivery driver and the goods-in clerk shared the proceeds of the stolen stock.

> ***Employees putting on weight***
>
> Employees at a major car manufacturer stole £2 million of spare parts by taping components to their bodies. A union agreement banned body searches. The parts were pooled and then sold to the public in bogus manufacturer's packaging.

In another case employees at a bulk plaster supplier stole plaster and sold it for cash to the local building trade, splitting the proceeds among factory employees as a 'bonus'. The plaster was loaded on to the lorries, weighed and appropriate delivery documentation produced. However, part of the load was unloaded at another warehouse used by the conspirators before it reached its destination. The fraud was not detected by the company's customers, who were small to medium-sized building contractors, because most did not have weighbridges and were content to have the plaster tipped into their silos or storage bins. They relied on the delivery note as confirming of the quantity delivered.

Warning signs include:

- unexplained differences between book and physical stock;
- stock turnover in particular locations inconsistent with the general level of turnover;
- poor margins or unusual fluctuations;
- delivery drivers driving part-loaded vehicles or asking for routes to be amended or asking to do the same routes; and
- deliveries received or made at unusual timés of the day.

The risk of this type of fraud is increased where there are:

- no monitoring of stock losses and no regular stock counts;
- weak goods received and despatch procedures;
- poor segregation of duties between buying, warehousing goods inward and accounting;

- poor control over stock movements at the time of stocktakes;
- poor control over unaccepted loads or incorrect loads; and
- no independent follow-up of customer complaints, for example re sub-standard products, delays in delivery or short deliveries.

Theft of returned stock or valuable scrap

Frauds involving returned stock or valuable scrap are also quite common. Rich pickings can be made by the opportunist fraudster.

For example, in one case partly damaged stock returned by customers to a building material manufacturer was removed by warehouse staff and sold to the public. In another case an employee at a manufacturing company who was responsible for sending high quality scrap metal to another company for reprocessing colluded with an employee at the processing company to falsify the weights and types of metal sent for reprocessing. The profits from the 'lost' metal were shared between the employees.

Metering and weighbridge frauds

Metering and weighbridge equipment are prone to tampering. Such equipment is crucial to the effective control of goods inward, despatch and stock taking. Regular checks on such equipment are therefore essential. Frequent breakdowns or faults occurring at unusual times should be regarded with suspicion and investigated thoroughly.

Detailed consideration of frauds involving metering and weighbridge equipment is outside the scope of this guide.

Manipulation of inventory records

Inventory records are often complex: for example, there may be transfers between manufacturing processes, numerous locations or a large number of stock lines. Such records are therefore an attractive place to conceal frauds either in inventory or in other areas.

Warning signs include:

- unexplained differences between book and physical stock;
- no detailed analysis of stock losses (by stock line, supplier, customer, delivery driver, warehouse staff, etc);
- stock lines with long turnover periods or abnormally large holdings of stock;

Improving an earnout

The directors of a company, which had been acquired by another group on earnout terms, capitalised costs in certain inventory accounts (not usually examined in detail) to improve a subsidiary's results. The amount was relatively small but multiplied by the earnout factor was highly significant.

- unexplained alterations to stock records or valuations;
- unusual number of credit notes or adjustments around period ends or the dates of stocktakes and unexplained items held in suspense accounts; and
- stock purported to be located in unusual or inaccessible places.

Cash and payment systems

As one would expect the scope for fraud and malpractice in the cash and payments area is huge. The most common types of fraud are listed below:

> ***Cash and payment systems***
>
> *Management and employee frauds*
>
> - Misuse of cheques and payment systems
> - Manipulation of bank reconciliations and cash books (*concealment devices*)
>
> *External frauds*
>
> - Money transfer frauds
> - Forged cheques

In addition to the above types of fraud, certain of the frauds discussed under *Dealing frauds* in Chapter 5 may also be relevant in larger groups which have sophisticated treasury operations.

Management and employee frauds

Misuse of cheques and payment systems

Some very large frauds have occurred in this area. Many more have been attempted. The boxed example below involved a payment of £23 million. Another attempted fraud, dressed up as a covert operation to secure the release of British hostages in the Middle East, involved an attempt to divert £40 million to a bank account in the Isle of Man.

Often these frauds are possible because the controls over the release of funds are inappropriate for the amounts involved. For example, at a financial institution processing was carried out by junior personnel and the final release of funds was dependent only on a check that the signatory was authorised to sign. This was insufficient for the amount involved ($70 million).

Warning signs include:

Attempt to divert £23 million

A senior accounts assistant in an oil company conspired to defraud the company of £23 million by seeking to divert an annual lease payment relating to an oil rig to a bank account in Switzerland. The accounts assistant stole the form authorising the transfer of the funds and substituted an international payment application directing the money to the Swiss bank account. An employee at the company's bank queried the payment application when he saw a message written on the top of the application urging the bank to make payment on time.

- poor security over cheques, cheque books and bank payment instructions;
- poor control over documents between approval and processing;
- management override of normal approval procedures;
- last minute requests for payment not supported by all the relevant documentation;
- abbreviated payee names, alterations to the date or payee, typed or handwritten details inserted on computer cheques;
- bank account through which cheque paid is different to account number on standing data; and
- unusual arrangements with banks for authorisation of transactions.

Other frauds involve the use of forged signatures, stolen cheques or cheque books, misuse of cancelled cheques, unsupported cash advances and the theft of cash or cash equivalents. For example, in one case an employee took three cheques from the back of an unused cheque book. The employee then forged the signatures on the cheques, making the cheques payable to a connected company. In another case the accounting function of a company's regional office was largely under the control of one person. The individual made unsupported cash advances to himself using old unclaimed credit balances to conceal the debit entries.

Further warning signs include:

- valuable documents or documents containing authorised signatures left unattended;
- weak procedures over the release of specimen signatures to banks;
- poor security over cancelled cheques;
- old or unidentified credits allowed to remain on ledger;
- no independent check on items going through suspense accounts; and
- bank mandates not accurate and up to date.

Further examples of frauds involving cheques and payment systems are included in the Digest of Cases.

Manipulation of bank reconciliations and cash books

Bank reconciliations are usually regarded as a strong control. However, such reconciliations must be properly prepared and subject to a thorough independent check from time to time to be effective. Cursory review and approval by management is not sufficient. A number of frauds would have been spotted if reconciliations had been completely reperformed periodically, for example during enforced holiday absence, and the details checked to other ledgers and supporting documentation.

> ***'Missing cheques . . .'***
>
> Two cheques were extracted from a cheque book and made payable to an individual, in whose name a bank account had been opened. The signature on the cheque was forged by copying authorised signatures from returned cheques. The cheques were entered in the cash book with the narrative 'missing cheques' against them so that the cheques would not appear on the bank reconciliations as reconciling items.

Concealment devices include:

- rolling matching;
- incorrect description of reconciling items;
- incorrect description of items in cash books; or
- the use of compensating debits and credits in other ledgers to make the bank reconciliation 'work'.

Rolling matching is the incorrect matching of items on reconciliations to facilitate the concealment of fraudulent items. It is most likely to happen when numerous items of a similar amount flow through an account.

Warning signs include:

- no independent detailed check of bank reconciliations – cursory review only;
- excessive numbers of contras and adjustments on reconciliations; and
- no review of endorsements or alterations on returned cheques.

Further examples of each of these devices are set out in the Digest of Cases.

External frauds

Money transfer fraud

Money transfer fraud involves the misuse of systems by external fraudsters to make fraudulent transfers of funds. Quite often these frauds involve collusion with management and employees. The frauds usually involve the misuse of passwords and authorisation codes or the forgery of documentation authorising transfers and are therefore closely related to the frauds discussed under *Misuse of cheques and payment systems* above. Similar frauds are also discussed under *Other external banking frauds* in the following chapter.

Warning signs include:

- transfers to or from accounts in offshore locations or countries with bank secrecy laws;
- transfers to or from individuals who are not regular suppliers;
- abbreviated payee names or alterations to the date, amount, payee or other details;
- poor control over documents between approval and processing;
- processing of significant transactions by junior personnel; and
- poor security over the room from which transfer instructions are issued or over codes and passwords.

Forged cheques

This type of fraud involves the theft of cheques or chequebooks or the manufacture of forged cheques by external fraudsters. The forgeries may be based on cheques, cancelled cheques or returned cheques and other documents containing authorised signatories. Alternatively the documents may be used to obtain chequebooks from the company's bankers. This type of fraud is widespread and is often conducted on a highly organised basis.

Possible warning signs are as for *Misuse of cheques and payment systems* above.

Other frauds

In this section we describe some of the other frauds which may affect companies:

Other frauds

Management and employee frauds

- Share support schemes
- Insider dealing
- Misuse of government grants/funding
- Misuse of pension funds and other assets
- Omitted contingencies
- Company car scheme frauds
- Payroll frauds
- Misuse of intercompany and suspense accounts (*concealment devices*)

External frauds

- Money laundering
- Bogus curriculum vitae
- Bogus insurance cover

Management and employee frauds

Share support schemes

There is a number of well-known cases where individuals in companies have used company funds to support the price of their own shares. The schemes often involve the use of offshore companies and other complex structures to conceal the identity of the purchaser. 'Consultancy' or other fees may also be paid to counterparties to purchase shares.

The motivation for such schemes is greatest when a company's share price is about to fall, maybe due to the announcement of poor trading results or some other factor such as the imminent departure of a key director/ shareholder with shares to sell. Another high risk scenario might be where a senior executive has a large share holding, lives expensively and has borrowed heavily on the shares of the company. Share support schemes may also be used when a company is about to make a significant acquisition, when the market price of the company's shares may be critical.

> ***Sub-underwriting your own share issue***
>
> Two directors of a company allegedly paid for millions of pounds of shares in their company by laundering company funds through private offshore companies set up for the purpose. One of the directors was a sub-underwriter for an issue of shares and used company funds to meet his obligations as underwriter.

It is difficult to identify possible warning signs for all the schemes which may be used. The financial position of the company, its trading performance, recent movements in its share prices, stock market conditions generally and any significant proposed transactions, such as a major acquisition, will usually be important. Any evidence of complex structures, including a pattern of purchases by offshore companies or transactions which are shrouded in secrecy, should be regarded with suspicion.

> ***Getting out while the going is good***
>
> The chairman of a quoted company sold a large holding of his company's shares just before an announcement of worse than expected figures, thereby avoiding a loss of approximately £1 million. Shortly afterwards the chairman resigned and trading in the company's shares was suspended. When trading resumed the shares traded at one-third of the original price. The chairman drew up a deed of gift, purporting to give his shares to his girlfriend – in fact he had authorised his bank to sell them after his resignation.

Insider dealing

Insider dealing is the improper use of unpublished price sensitive information by certain individuals when dealing in a quoted company's shares. Detailed consideration of insider dealing and the various criminal charges is outside the scope of this guide. However, typical scenarios include directors of a company dealing in the company's shares prior to the announcement of worse than expected results or before the announcement of a takeover bid, or consultants and advisers of the company dealing in the company's shares based on similar unpublished price sensitive information. Insider dealing offences also relate to others to whom unpublished price sensitive information has been divulged.

Most quoted companies have strict rules concerning dealings in the company's shares. Similarly merchant bank, accountants, lawyers and other advisers tend to have strict rules concerning share dealings in companies for whom they are acting. Clearly the absence of such rules or staff who are not fully conversant with the rules should cause concern.

Misuse of government grants/funding

As with share support and insider dealing frauds, this type of fraud often involves the use of complex structures to conceal the fraud. The risk of this type of fraud is greatest when a company is in a perilous financial position or when trading conditions are difficult.

> ***A black hole***
>
> Directors of two companies channelled several million pounds of government funding and loans relating to a major project through a Panamanian-registered Swiss-based company for their own use.

Possible warning signs are:

- transactions handled exclusively by a director which are shrouded in secrecy;
- no clear accountability for government funding received; and
- complex structures of offshore companies.

Misuse of pension funds or other assets

Pension funds and other assets may be used to bail out ailing companies. In recent years there has been a number of cases where pension fund assets have been stolen or used as security to obtain loans. In other cases assets have been transferred from the employing company to the pension fund at above their market value.

> ***Bailing out a 'sinking ship'***
>
> The chief executive of a construction company which was in financial difficulties allegedly stole a cheque for nearly £1 million and shares in various quoted companies from the group's pension fund.

Warning signs include:

- access to assets created through legal arrangements – for example, powers of attorney, investment management agreements and trustee companies;

- pension fund has different accounting period from employer; and
- transfers of assets between employing company and the pension fund where the market value cannot be readily ascertained.

Omitted contingencies

Omitted contingency frauds involve the use of undisclosed guarantees, commitments and other contingencies to improve the apparent financial position of a company. Companies in a parlous financial position are high risk. Other frauds in this area include the pledging of assets of the company as security for borrowing for private or associated companies where the funds can be stripped. These frauds have been prevalent in the banking industry (discussed further in Chapter 5). They are easy to commit and easy to conceal.

> ***Taking profits early***
>
> Due to poor trading results, a company gave a side letter to a customer setting out certain undertakings, in consideration for the issue of a completion certificate. This enabled profit to be taken early on the contract even though certain contractual obligations had not been completed.

Warning signs of this type of fraud include:

- unexpected completions ahead of schedule; or
- unusual trends in results in the period prior to the year end.

Company car scheme frauds

Company car scheme frauds usually involve the sale of ex-fleet cars to connected parties at discount prices. External frauds include overbilling for labour on servicing or repairs, in particular where the invoice is passed directly to the employing company (i.e., not inspected by the employee). Some examples of company car scheme frauds are included in the Digest of Cases.

Warning signs include:

- no independent checks on the prices at which, and the parties to whom, company cars are sold;
- same purchaser for a range of models; and
- single source of supply for key services such as repairs.

These points are of particular importance in self-insured fleets.

Payroll frauds

Payroll frauds involve the use of dummy employees, unauthorised increases to salaries and bogus commissions, bonuses and overtime payments. The risk of such frauds is particularly high when segregation of duties is poor and where there are remote locations poorly supervised.

Warning signs include:

- no checks on bonuses, commissions and overtime payments;
- employees not on voters' register; and
- no zero based budgets.

The phantom of the factory

A manager at a remote plant, where there was a large number of employees, was responsible for submitting time cards and summary sheets for employees. He input details for a dummy employee over a three-year period.

Misuse of intercompany and suspense accounts (concealment devices)

Intercompany accounts and suspense accounts are often used to conceal frauds. Intercompany accounts in large groups may not be reconciled regularly or items may be incorrectly described as 'timing differences' when in fact there is a discrepancy – i.e., one set of books is wrong.

Suspense accounts also require careful scrutiny. It is important to review the nature of items passing through suspense accounts during the year (including 'contra' items) even if the account is cleared to zero at the year end. Review of the activity on suspense accounts may reveal unusual patterns of entries.

An unreconciled account

The chairman of a company concealed payments for his own account by arranging for the payments to be debited in the holding company books in its account with a foreign subsidiary – the account was not properly reconciled.

Sometimes suspense accounts are used when none are needed. This enables fraudsters to shift fraudulent items between various accounts, creating a complex web of entries to cover their tracks.

Warning signs include:

- intercompany accounts not reconciled and adjustments not posted (all differences treated as 'timing' differences) especially accounts which are not strictly intercompany i.e., with associates or related parties outside the group;
- reasons for transactions, particularly with overseas companies, unclear or shrouded in secrecy;
- high volume of items passing through suspense accounts, even if apparently cleared at the year end; and
- large round sum cash movements.

External frauds

Money laundering

Money laundering is an extremely important issue for many businesses, particularly those in the financial sector. The Joint Money Laundering Steering Group issued detailed guidance notes in October 1993 to assist businesses in the financial sector prepare for the changes in the law included in the Criminal Justice Act 1993. These guidance notes also include more general guidance on money laundering. This part of the chapter is based closely on those notes. Readers are encouraged to consult the guidance notes themselves.

Money laundering is the process by which criminals attempt to conceal the true origin and ownership of the proceeds of their criminal activities. If undertaken successfully, it also allows them to maintain control over the proceeds and, ultimately, to provide a legitimate cover for their source of income.

> **A bogus property company**
>
> Drug traffickers importing cannabis from West Africa employed a solicitor who set up a client account. The solicitor deposited £500,000 received from them, later transferring the funds to his firm's bank account. Subsequently, acting on instructions, the solicitor withdrew the funds from the account and used them to purchase a number of properties on behalf of the drug traffickers.

The need to launder the proceeds of criminal activity through the financial system is vital to the success of criminal operations. Therefore most of the effort to combat money laundering focuses on those points in the process where the launderer's activities are more susceptible to recognition and have therefore tended to concentrate on the deposit taking procedures of banks and building societies. However, there are many schemes where cash is not involved and quite a wide range of businesses, outside the financial sector, may be used to launder funds.

There is no one method of laundering money. Methods range from the purchase and resale of a valuable item (for example, a luxury car, jewellery, works of art or even gold bars) to passing money through a complex international web of legitimate businesses and 'shell' companies. Initially, however, in many instances the proceeds usually take the form of cash which needs to enter the financial system by some means.

The laundering process is usually described as taking place in three stages:

- placement – the physical disposal of cash proceeds derived from illegal activity;
- layering – separating illicit proceeds from their source by creating

complex layers of financial transactions designed to disguise the audit trail and provide anonymity;

- integration – the provision of apparent legitimacy to criminally derived wealth. If the layering process has succeeded integration schemes place the laundered proceeds back into the economy in such a way that they re-enter the financial system appearing as normal business funds.

The above three steps may well overlap or occur simultaneously. Typical examples of the activities at each stage are set out in the table below:

Theft of company funds

The director of a wholesale supply company issued cheques to third parties which were deposited into their respective bank accounts, both in the United Kingdom and with offshore banks. Cheques drawn on the third party accounts were handed back to the director made payable to him personally and were paid into his personal bank account. False company invoices were raised purporting to show the supply of goods by third parties to the company.

Examples of money laundering activity

Placement stage	*Layering stage*	*Integration stage*
Cash paid into bank (sometimes with staff complicity or mixed with proceeds of legitimate business)	Wire transfers abroad (often using 'shell' companies or funds disguised as proceeds of legitimate business)	False loan repayments or forged invoices used as cover for laundered money
Cash exported	Cash deposited in overseas banking system	Complex web of transfers (both domestic and international) making tracing original source of funds virtually impossible
Cash used to buy high value goods, property or business assets	Resale of goods/assets	Income from property or legitimate business assets appears 'clean'

Businesses especially vulnerable to money laundering are cash-based businesses such as restaurants and casinos or any business dealing in high value portable items, such as jewellery and art. However, as indicated above, there are many other methods, involving complex international webs of legitimate businesses and 'shell' companies.

Guidance on money laundering in banking, investment business and insurance is included in Chapter 5.

Bogus curriculum vitae

Many companies do not have effective recruitment screening procedures. Sometimes fraudsters have committed similar frauds in their previous employments.

Items on job applications or matters which come up during interview may give a clue. For example, in one case a credit controller indicated on her job application that she was a qualified chartered accountant. In fact, she had never taken any of the exams. She had committed exactly the same fraud in her three previous employments but none of the companies checked the register of members. If this item had been checked it might have put the companies on notice that all was not well.

Warning signs include:

- references not checked;
- inconsistencies or gaps in employment history not followed up;
- grandiose claims; and
- attempts to mislead, contradictory answers, extreme defensiveness or excessive bravado when questioned about certain matters.

Personnel policies are discussed in Chapter 7.

> ***The man for the job***
>
> An individual who had already served a four-year prison sentence for obtaining property by deception obtained a job claiming he had a triple honours MBA, fluency in Mandarin, Chinese and Japanese and a glowing reference from a Home Office minister. The CV and the reference were completely bogus.

Bogus insurance cover

> ***Not worth the paper it's written on***
>
> A company which offered extended insurance guarantees on electrical appliances defrauded a number of major companies of more than £6 million by issuing bogus insurance warranties. The company used photocopying machines to create bogus documents, which were passed off as five-year extended insurance gurantees.

Cases have been reported of bogus insurance policies being offered to companies by insurance intermediaries. These frauds usually involve the forgery of insurance documentation of well-known insurance companies.

Warning signs include:

- quality of documentation below the standard expected;
- unusually low insurance premiums; and
- intermediary ensures that all contact with the insurer is via him.

Fraud in the public sector

In many respects frauds in the public sector mirror those in the private sector. Most of the frauds discussed in this chapter could take place in the public sector, albeit sometimes in a slightly different form. However, certain types of frauds are particularly prevalent in the public sector and therefore we give further examples of these types of fraud below:

> ***Further examples of fraud in the public sector***
>
> *Management and employee frauds*
>
> - Underbilling/underringing
> - Kickbacks and inducements
>
> *External frauds*
>
> - Sub-standard products
> - Billing for work not performed/overbilling
> - False claims for grants/benefits

Management and employee frauds

Underbilling/underringing

As noted under *Sales* above, underbilling and underringing is a widespread problem not only in the retail sector but also in other industries. In the public sector there are a wide range of situations where weaknesses in ticket systems, toll gates or other sales systems can be exploited by the fraudster. A typical example is shown opposite.

> ***A heavy toll***
>
> 18 employees defrauded a local authority of £1 million over five years relating to tunnel tolls. One individual earning £10,000 a year ran three cars and owned a boat and a caravan. The fraudsters together siphoned off about £11,000 a week.

Kickbacks and inducements

Kickbacks and inducements are a major problem in the public sector. This is partly due to the size and number of contracts awarded. Many contracts are extremely lucrative. Also the cash-based nature of much government budgeting may leave gaps near the year end. Efforts to ensure all the budget is spent may result in both internal and external fraud.

There have been numerous cases over the years. For example, three British Rail managers took bribes from a garage owner worth hundreds of thousands of pounds, including foreign holidays and cash, in return for awarding road vehicle maintenance contracts. An environmental health officer passed lists of home owners applying for home improvement grants to a double-glazing salesman and was paid commission on the contracts obtained.

Eleven officials of a government agency received cash, foreign holidays, the services of call girls, home improvements and clothing in return for handing out lucrative contracts to builders for the maintenance of royal palaces, laboratories, law courts and government offices. The chief executive of a munitions company gave a BMW and a holiday in Florida to an MOD official as an inducement to win contracts for the supply of mortars and ammunition.

External frauds

Sub-standard products

> **_Garden rubbish burns well . . ._**
>
> Four directors of a company which was supposed to supply high grade blended coal worth £36 per ton to a power station supplied inferior coal worth £4.60 per ton and, on occasion, garden rubbish. The fraudsters paid three power station samplers £1,200 per week. The fraud was discovered when output from the power station dropped by 6 per cent due to the low quality fuel.

As noted under *Purchases* above, sub-standard product frauds are quite common. As with *Kickbacks and inducements* above, the prevalence of this type of fraud in the public sector is largely due to the size and number of contracts awarded. The risk of such fraud is greatly increased where quality control checks are weak, where there are no independent checks on the credentials or capabilities of key suppliers, where suppliers are changed at the last minute or where there are 'rushed jobs'.

Billing for work not performed/ overbilling

We noted under *Purchases* above that contracts most susceptible to this kind of fraud are ones where large numbers of invoices are submitted, the service is supplied at a remote location or checking the performance at various stages of the contract is difficult. Such frauds are reported to be very common in the public sector.

False claims for grants/benefits

> ***Bogus companies claim RDGs***
>
> An individual formed three companies and claimed he had created 79 new jobs. In fact the companies never operated. He had obtained the 79 names at random from job centres together with the individuals' national insurance numbers. He obtained £200,000 of Regional Development Grants.

Grant and benefit fraud is a particular problem in the public sector. This type of fraud has some similarities to the insurance claim frauds discussed in Chapter 5. The frauds often involve fictitious applicants or bogus companies. Alternatively the amount of the claim may be overstated or the reason for the claim misstated.

In certain cases forgery is involved, for example forgery of pension allowance books used at post offices. In one case six individuals ran a nationwide counterfeiting operation and obtained £3.6 million using forged pension allowance books.

Conclusion

> ***Charity begins at home***
>
> The director of a charity allegedly obtained £400,000 in grants from a council and a government department. He used the money to buy a hotel in Barbados for his retirement.

All of the frauds discussed in this chapter are very common. They occur again and again, albeit in slightly different forms. Companies need to ensure that they are well protected against these core risks. Certain types of fraud are highly visible, for example major thefts of cash or stock. However, many others, for example those involving kickbacks and inducements, are more difficult to detect. It may not be clear that the company has suffered a loss. It is therefore crucial to be alert to the warning signs of fraud which may provide the first clue that there is a problem.

5 FRAUD IN THE FINANCIAL SECTOR

Introduction

Companies in the financial sector are susceptible to many of the frauds described in the previous chapter. These are general types of fraud which may affect virtually any company. However, the financial sector is also subject to a large number of more specialised frauds. Some of these frauds are similar to frauds in other sectors but for the most part they are best understood in the context of particular businesses in the financial sector. Some are unique to those businesses. In this chapter we examine frauds in banking, investment business, insurance and leasing. As in the previous chapter it is important to consider the 'indicators of fraud' discussed in Chapter 2 alongside the guidance given in this chapter.

Banking

Frauds in banks fall into four main areas:

- lending;
- deposit taking;
- dealing; and
- other areas.

As in the previous chapter, we identify the key phases in each business cycle and the points at which the risk of fraud is greatest.

LENDING

There are three main phases in the lending cycle:

- introduction and appraisal of the borrower;
- taking security and the release of funds; and
- payment of interest, repayment of the loan principal and the release of security.

In the first phase of the cycle, introduction and appraisal of the borrower, the main concerns relate to the identity of the borrower, his financial status, who introduced the borrower and on what terms. Typical management and employee frauds in this phase of the cycle include the creation of fictitious loans or the granting of loans to connected borrowers, usually disguised by the use of nominee or 'front' companies.

Lending to connected borrowers may also be disguised by what is known as 'deposit transformation': the fraudster places a deposit with a 'friendly' bank, which in turn lends the money, against the security of the deposit, to a nominated beneficiary of the fraudster. Management may also approve loans in which they have an undisclosed interest, for example through joint venture or profit sharing arrangements.

Management may seek to conceal the extent of lending to particular borrowers so that they appear to meet regulatory requirements or may disguise the identity of certain borrowers to conceal their credit status. Management and employees may also be bribed by borrowers to obtain credit. External frauds include impersonation and the submission of false information on loan applications.

In the second stage of the cycle, taking security and the release of funds, the key concerns relate to the nature and value of the security, ensuring that there is no release of funds before appropriate security is taken, and whether the loan funds are used by the customer for the purpose for which they were intended. Typical management frauds include using the bank's own funds to provide collateral for its lending. External frauds include double pledging of collateral by borrowers, land flips (involving sales between connected parties to boost valuations artificially for collateral purposes), fraudulent valuations, the use of forged or valueless collateral, loan funds used for a different purpose than that indicated on the loan application and misappropriation of loan funds by solicitors and agents.

In the third stage of the cycle, payment of interest, repayment of the loan and the release of security, the main concerns are that payments are made in accordance with the loan agreement and that the payments are in fact made by the borrower. Where a problem arises with the payment of either interest or principal, management may seek to give a false impression of the financial soundness of particular borrowers, to avoid making provisions or to meet regulatory requirements. The fraudster may achieve this by generating false activity on loan accounts, usually by circulating the bank's own money or depositors' funds and 'transforming' the funds into an apparent repayment from the borrower. Alternatively, management may transfer problem loans to other parts of the group, where they may be subject to less scrutiny by auditors or regulators. Loans may also be transferred to connected parties with an agreement to repurchase at some future date. External frauds include bribes paid to management or employees to obtain the release of the security before the loan is repaid.

Finally, sales of recovered security are often poorly controlled and offer internal fraudsters opportunities to profit personally. In one case, a bank credit officer even arranged loans to co-conspirators to purchase such assets at prices much lower than their market values.

The above frauds are illustrated in the following chart:

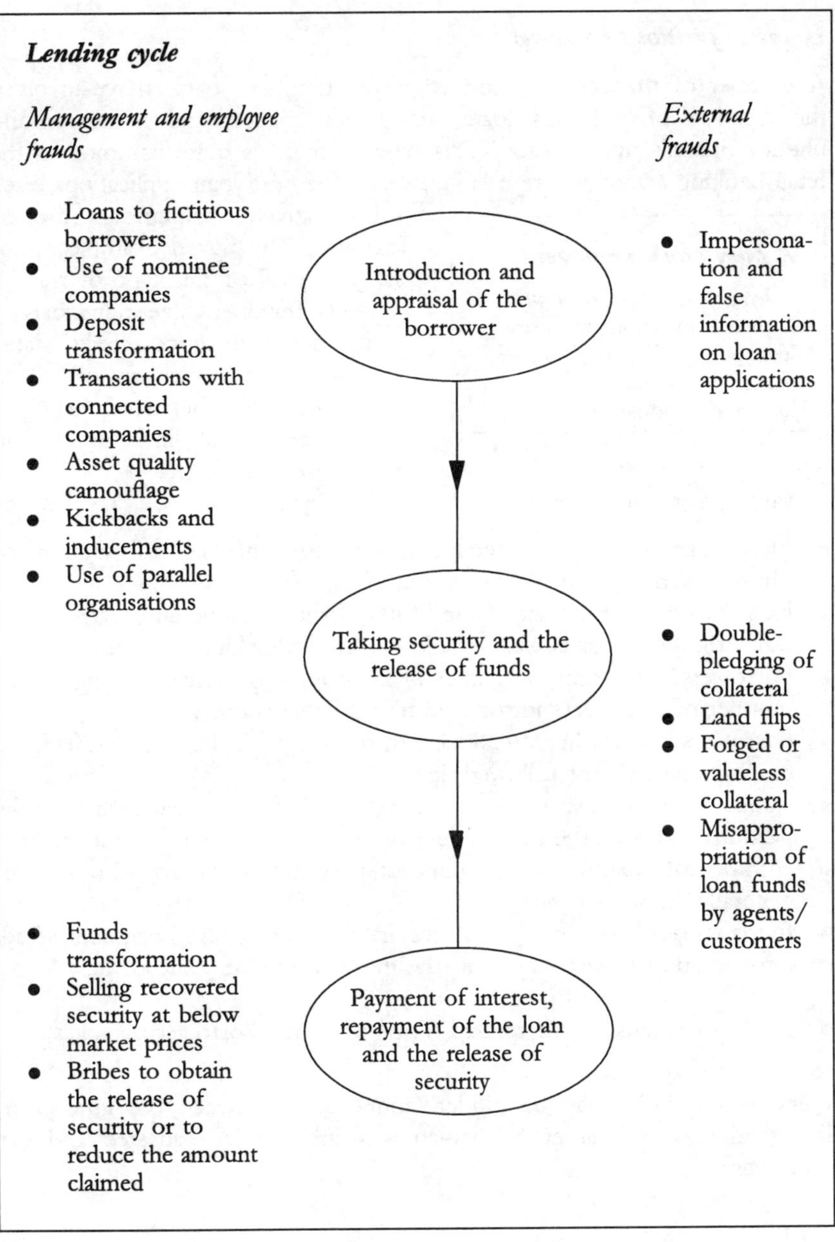

Management and employee frauds

Loans to fictitious borrowers

A number of management and employee frauds in banks have involved the creation of fictitious loans, using false names and addresses and phoney financial information. This type of fraud is quite common in the retail banking sector where a large number of false loan applications, each for a relatively small amount, may be involved. The boxed example opposite is typical of this type of fraud.

> ***A busy bank manager***
>
> A branch manager of a well-known bank arranged false loans amounting to £260,000, using 70 false names on bogus loan applications.

Other frauds involve individuals or companies with good credit status 'lending' their names to others to obtain loans, in other words acting as 'front men', usually in return for an undisclosed payment.

Warning signs include:

- 'thin' loan files with sketchy, incomplete financial information or photocopied or scrappy documentation;
- loans or overdrafts where there is little documentation and management claim the borrower is wealthy and his 'creditworthiness is undoubted';
- borrowers with common names or like-sounding names or a significant number of borrowers introduced by the same source;
- borrowers not on the voters' register, missing credit checks or references or discrepancies not followed up;
- valuations which seem high, valuers used from outside the usually permitted area or the same valuer used on numerous applications;
- commercial customers or significant personal borrowers who are not generally known to staff;
- funds released before all the necessary formalities have been completed;
- remuneration closely linked to the number and/or value of new loans; and
- generous extensions or revised terms when the borrower defaults.

Quite often there may be hidden connections between the introducer, the vendor of the asset for which loan finance is requested and the borrower.

Use of nominee companies

Other more sophisticated devices are used to conceal fictitious or connected lending. Rather than lend funds in personal names the fraudster may seek to disguise the borrowing through offshore companies or trustee or management arrangements.

Files kept outside the main filing system or documentation kept in the offices of senior officials which apparently does not relate to the institution should be regarded with suspicion. Similarly, evasive replies concerning particular loans or when access to such documentation is requested may provide a clue to such arrangements.

> ***Personal papers***
>
> The managing director at a bank made a loan to himself via an offshore company owned by him. The loan file implied that the company was owned by one of the director's contacts rather than the director himself. Other documents, which revealed the true nature of the loan, were kept in his office.

Warning signs include:

- 'thin' loan files with sketchy or incomplete financial information;
- loans to individuals or companies in remote jurisdictions, outside the area of the bank's or branch's normal operations;
- loans to offshore companies with no clear business purpose;
- complex structures which are shrouded in secrecy;
- few details on file about the individuals behind particular companies or arrangements;
- a strong recommendation from a senior official at the bank but few other details to support the loan;
- like-sounding names between borrowers; and
- sole contact customers (i.e., handled exclusively by one member of staff).

Deposit transformation

A further way in which management may disguise connected lending is to make the loan at one remove by what we call 'deposit transformation'. This involves the fraudster placing a deposit with another bank which in turn lends money to a nominated beneficiary of the fraudster against the security of the deposit. No record of the pledge or the contingent liability arising in respect of the ultimate loan is made, thereby not only concealing the credit exposure but also retaining the benefit of the deposit to satisfy liquidity reporting requirements. This type of fraud has featured in many of the major banking frauds we have encountered in the last twenty years.

Warning signs include:

- pledges over deposits (disclosed by confirmations which have specifically requested such pledges to be disclosed);
- deposits which are continually rolled over;
- long-term deposits placed when liquidity is tight;
- unusual counterparties;

> ***An unusual strategy***
>
> An overseas bank with liquidity problems made substantial medium-term deposits with a disreputable bank when the funds were urgently required to meet pressing commitments. It transpired that the deposits had been used by the disreputable bank to secure lending by that bank to a company related to the directors.

- documentation or files held in directors' or senior managers' offices outside the usual filing areas;
- evasive replies when access to such documents is requested; and
- weak controls over the giving and recording of guarantees.

Transactions with connected companies

Certain loans may appear to be to third-party borrowers. However, joint venture agreements or profit sharing arrangements, from which a director or senior official of the bank may benefit (on an undisclosed basis), may be linked to the loan. Usually the loan would not have been entered into but for the hidden arrangement.

The possible warning signs of this type of fraud are as for *Loans to fictitious borrowers* and *Use of nominee companies.* Other tell-tale signs are jottings on files which are not consistent with other information on file (e.g., names, addresses, telephone numbers of unknown individuals) and repayments made by persons other than the borrower.

> ***An attractive lending opportunity***
>
> The chief executive of a bank approved a loan regarding the development of a golf and country club. There was an undisclosed side arrangement whereby he would receive 30 per cent of the profit from the development. Files relating to the arrangement were kept in his office, separate from the main loan files.

Asset quality camouflage

Management may need to conceal the extent of lending to particular borrowers, either to avoid provisions or to meet regulatory requirements. Asset quality camouflage involves various forms of manipulation designed to enhance, artificially, the apparent quality of assets. These frauds are often closely linked to *Funds transformation* frauds below.

Possible warning signs as for *Use of nominee companies.*

> ***Large exposures***
>
> The chief executive of a bank agreed with a particular borrower that the finance for a series of very large projects should be spread between a large number of offshore companies. The ownership of the companies was disguised so that the true extent of the lending to the customer was concealed.

Kickbacks and inducements

Borrowers may offer bribes to management and employees to obtain credit or to manipulate lending criteria. The risk of this type of fraud is increased where the remuneration of loan officers is closely linked to the number or value of new loans entered into.

Warning signs include:

- excessive amounts of business generated by particular loan officers;
- lending criteria overridden regularly by particular loan officers;
- sole contact customers;
- concentration of lending in particular sectors or through particular sources of introduction;
- change in pattern of business towards high risk areas; and
- strong recommendation by director or lending officer but missing data or documentation on credit file.

Use of parallel organisations

'Parallel organisations' are companies under common control of the directors and/or shareholders. Such companies are often used in *Asset camouflage* frauds and *Funds transformation* (see below). However, they may also be used for other purposes, for example, undisclosed sale and repurchase agreements, circular refinancing arrangements and sales at other than market value.

Warning signs include:

- unexpected settlement of problem loans shortly before the period end or prior to an audit visit;
- unexpected new lending close to the period end;
- transfers of loans, especially to companies which are suspected to have some connection with the directors and/or shareholders;
- poor controls over the giving and recording of guarantees or similar commitments;
- transactions or structures shrouded in secrecy;
- changes in the pattern of business with related organisations.

> ***Pressing personal needs***
>
> A bank made a short-term loan to an individual overseas to meet 'pressing personal needs'. The loan was secured by a cash deposit from an offshore company. In fact the individual was a friend of the managing director, who had incurred large gambling debts. The offshore company was owned by the managing director and the funds placed in the deposit account were drawn by the managing director from other customers' funds held on long term deposit or under hold-mail arrangements.

Parallel organisations may also be used to secure the bank's own lending. This is usually achieved by a series of transactions which result in the bank's own funds being transferred into offshore companies, which are ostensibly third party depositors. The funds deposited in these accounts are then used as cash collateral for the lending.

> ***Passing the parcel***
>
> A bank transferred loans to a subsidiary audited by another firm before its year end with an unrecorded arrangement to repurchase the loans at face value after its year end.

Funds transformation

When it is likely that a borrower may default on a loan, management may seek to give a false impression of the financial soundness of the borrower. This may be to avoid making provisions or to satisfy regulatory requirements. 'Funds transformation' involves concealment of the nature or source of funds. For example, the bank's own funds may be routed, via subsidiaries, branches, associated companies or companies under common ownership, to 'transform' the funds into an apparent repayment from the borrower. Sometimes the loans involved may be connected with the directors or staff of the bank in some way or set up for some fraudulent purpose.

Warning signs include:

- sources of receipt which are inconsistent with the standing data;
- loans which suddenly become current shortly before the period end or prior to an audit visit;
- transactions with companies within a group or with its associated companies where the business purpose is unclear;
- unusual arrangements involving offshore companies and/or companies under common ownership;
- annotations on file which do not appear to relate to the borrower (e.g., names, addresses, telephone numbers and other jottings); and
- files kept outside the normal filing areas.

> ***Round the houses***
>
> A bank made a loan to purchase a property development undertaken by the chairman's brother-in-law. The loan was non-performing and there was a shortfall on the security. The bank transferred an amount equal to the shortfall through a branch, subsidiary and an associated institution under its management and back to the bank as though they were a receipt from the chairman's brother-in-law.

Selling recovered security at below market prices

Many banks have strong credit procedures and controls relating to the main part of the credit cycle. However, procedures and controls may be much less rigorous in situations where the borrower has defaulted and the bank is in possession of the recovered security. Checks over the prices at which and the parties to whom such assets are sold are sometimes very weak providing the opportunity for officers of the bank to obtain hidden profits or kickbacks.

Bribes to obtain the release of security or to reduce the amount claimed

Just as bribes may be paid to loan officers to obtain credit in the first place, so they may be paid by borrowers to obtain the release of security before the loan principal has been repaid. Bribes may also encourage loan officers to reduce their banks' claims after the loan is in default.

External frauds

Impersonation and false information on loan applications

Impersonation and the submission of false information on loan applications is a significant external threat for any bank. Banks most vulnerable to this type of activity are those with inexperienced loan officers or where appraisal of loans is largely a desk top review. Vulnerability to this type of fraud is high during periods of rapid growth when banks may be keen to gain market share.

Another aspect which is crucial at the appraisal stage is assessing who the introducer of the business is and how well he knows the borrower. In quite a number of cases the bank may think that the introducer, for example a firm of solicitors or accountants, knows the customer well. This might not always be the case. The borrower may be a recent acquaintance. It is also important to look at concentrations of business obtained from introducers, in particular loan brokers, and possible personal or business connections between the introducer and personnel of the bank.

Examples of false information on loan applications include:

- grandiose claims concerning the borrower's business credentials: for example, a borrower, who requested a loan for the purchase and refurbishment of a hotel, claimed to have extensive experience of the hotel industry whereas he had never owned or run a hotel;
- false accounts: a borrower falsified a set of audited accounts; the accounts appeared genuine in every way, except the source and application of funds statement did not add up; and
- false accounting records or other

> **Mr Money**
>
> An undischarged bankrupt and convicted fraudster posed as an international lawyer and a duke. He entertained the manager of a well-known bank at Claridges. The manager opened 25 bank accounts for the man, nicknamed Mr Money. When the overdraft facilities were exhausted, Mr Money loaded his Rolls Royce with art treasures and fled to his chateau in France.

data relating to the business: for example, directors of an ailing toy manufacturing company used fake computer records of sales to convince banks and finance companies to lend them money.

Warning signs include:

- grandiose claims not corroborated;
- extravagant lifestyle or lavish entertaining of bank officials by the customer;
- no on-site appraisal of borrower;
- business ventures too good to be true;
- inexperienced loan officers;
- sole contact customers; and
- difficulty in obtaining corroboration of the individual's credentials, inconsistent or missing documentation and inconsistencies in personal details (such as voter's register and credit status checks).

Double-pledging of collateral/land flips/forged or valueless collateral

Many external frauds against banks involve the use of false or misvalued security, for example, the double pledging of collateral, forged or valueless collateral or collateral whose value has been inflated. The latter problem often involves what are known as 'land flips'. These are sales of property between connected parties (usually there is a series of such sales) to boost artificially the valuation of the property for collateral purposes.

Other frauds involve bribes paid to valuers to obtain false valuations. The certificates of other professionals, for example architects' certificates in connection with refurbishment work, are sometimes forged or overstated. The risk of this type of fraud is greatly increased where there are no on-site visits by the bank's staff. For example, in one case if such a visit had been made to the hotel concerned it would have been apparent that although refurbishment work was being undertaken it was at a much lower cost than indicated in the loan application.

Warning signs are as for *Impersonation/false information on loan applications* above. Other possible warning signs include:

- valuer from outside the area in which the property is situated;

> **_A development in Docklands_**
>
> Seven people connected with a redevelopment in Docklands, including estate agents and solicitors, allegedly arranged for the initial buyers of flats which were being built to resell their properties to various offshore companies at false market valuations. An overseas bank lent to new buyers on the basis of these valuations assuming that they were open market prices obtained for the properties.

> ***Bogus share certificates***
>
> Three businessmen allegedly attempted to defraud one of the major clearing banks of £3 million by using forged share certificates, supposedly worth £7 million, as collateral for a loan.

- same valuer used in a large number of transactions;
- same valuer used by both parties;
- series of sales of a particular asset over a short period with values increasing on each sale;
- identity of principals difficult to ascertain/use of nominee or 'front' companies; and
- borrower known to have access to substantial assets (for example, pension fund assets) of a type similar to those pledged.

Misappropriation of loan funds by agents/customers

This type of fraud involves the misuse of loan funds by customers, borrowers or their agents, for example in one case short-term loans obtained to finance international trade were used to fund long-term loans to two virtually bankrupt companies overseas. In another case involving a solicitor funds ostensibly for clients' bridging loans were diverted by the solicitor into his firm's account.

Warning signs are as for *Impersonation/false information on loan applications* above.

DEPOSIT TAKING

The deposit taking cycle may be analysed into three key phases, as follows:

- verifying the identity of the depositor and establishing the source of the funds;
- recording the funds deposited; and
- handling the funds in accordance with the customer's instructions.

Verifying the identity of new customers and establishing the source of the funds deposited is a key requirement for any bank. The main concern is money laundering. Consideration of the legal requirements and the various practical matters which banks should address in relation to money laundering is outside the scope of this guide. As already noted, detailed guidance on these matters is provided in notes issued by the Joint Money Laundering Steering Group.

In some cases management may collude with depositors to disguise their identity. For example, false names or code names may be used to conceal the identity of customers.

The next phase in the deposit taking cycle is the proper recording of the funds deposited. A number of international banking frauds have involved the diversion of deposits to bank accounts controlled by the fraudster (i.e., the deposits are never recorded in the bank's books). Banks most susceptible to this type of fraud are those operating hold-mail arrangements and those taking long-term deposits from overseas customers who are rarely in contact with the bank.

The third phase of the cycle involves handling deposits in accordance with the customer's instructions. This involves proper segregation of the customer's funds and ensuring that transfers from deposit accounts, or sales of customer investments, are made in accordance with properly authorised instructions. Typical management and employee frauds in this area involve the merging of depositor and personal funds and the theft of customer funds or investments. External frauds include the use of fraudulent payment instructions.

The above frauds are illustrated on the following chart:

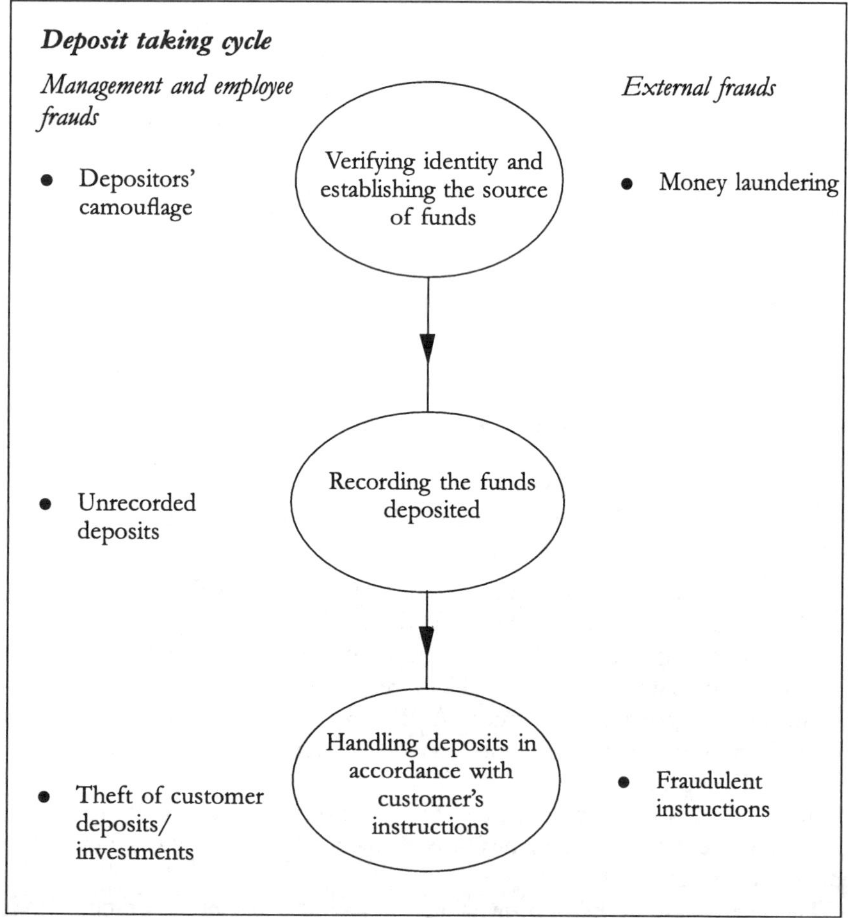

Management and employee frauds

Depositors' camouflage

As noted above, management may collude with a depositor to conceal his identity through the use of false names or code names. A large number of such names may be used. Management may also set up accounts themselves using false names or code names to conceal their interest in certain accounts.

Often this will be because the funds which are being deposited are the proceeds of criminal conduct. However, there may be other reasons why the identity of certain depositors may be disguised. For example, a bank may wish to conceal the extent to which its deposit base derives from a particular source or certain depositors may be directors of the bank or their associates or even the bank's own funds used to secure lending to nominated beneficiaries of the directors.

> ***The MD in disguise***
>
> Several accounts at a bank overseas were in fact the managing director and principal shareholder in disguise. Some accounts had like-sounding names. Others were in the names of offshore companies owned by the managing director.

Warning signs include:

- similar or like-sounding names across various accounts;
- offshore company depositors with no clearly defined business or about which there are few details; and
- depositor files with little information on them, particularly where they are resident in countries associated with drugs trafficking or terrorist activities.

Unrecorded deposits

A number of major international banking frauds in recent years have involved the diversion of deposits to accounts controlled by the fraudster. Usually the funds are not recorded in the bank's books at all, the deposits being routed through intermediaries or by the bank paying away receipts without recording the receipt or the payment in the accounting records. Often the accounts to which the funds are diverted are located in offshore locations or countries with strict bank secrecy laws.

This type of fraud is most likely to occur when certain of the bank's depositors are resident overseas and/or where funds are held on long-term deposit or under hold-mail arrangements. As a result the customer may not be in regular contact with the bank and may not receive statements. The risk of this type of fraud is increased where the depositors concerned seek to remove their funds from an oppressive home jurisdiction. The depositors may put a higher level of trust in the bank concerned to make the necessary arrangements and take care of the money deposited.

Warning signs include:

- any evidence of deposit taking by any other company of which there are details on the premises, whether part of the regulated group or not;
- documentation held in management offices which it is claimed has no connection with the business of the bank; and
- evasive replies regarding such documents.

Deposits re-routed to fund personal activities

A director of an overseas bank took deposits from certain overseas customers into code-numbered accounts in a Swiss bank. He had sole contact with most of the customers, who mostly wished to hold their funds on long-term deposit outside the home jurisdiction. The funds were moved from the Swiss bank into other off-shore accounts and used by the director to fund various of his other interests.

Theft of customer deposits/investments

Where customers are not in regular contact with a bank or where a high level of discretion is extended to the bank by the customer, the scope for the misuse of customers' funds or investments is increased. The example opposite is typical of the circumstances in which this type of fraud may occur.

This type of fraud is different to *Unrecorded deposits* above because the customer's funds or assets will have been recorded in the bank's books initially, only later being misused.

Warning signs include:

- customers with hold-mail arrangements who only have very occasional contact with the bank; and
- no independent resolution of customer complaints or review of hold mail accounts.

Gambling with customers' money

A branch manager stole £730,000 from a customer's account while the customer was being 'detained' overseas. The manager had been given authority to make investments on the customer's behalf during the customer's absence. However, he spent the money on gambling.

External frauds

Money laundering

We discussed in the previous chapter the three main stages of money laundering and some typical examples of the activity at each stage. Banks and building societies are of course especially vulnerable to money laundering not only at the placement stage through deposit taking but also in the layering and integration stages. For example, mortgage and other loan accounts may be used as part of this process to create complex layers of transactions.

The aim of the criminal is to convert the proceeds of criminal activities from 'dirty money' into 'clean money'. The chart below shows a common way in which this might be done.

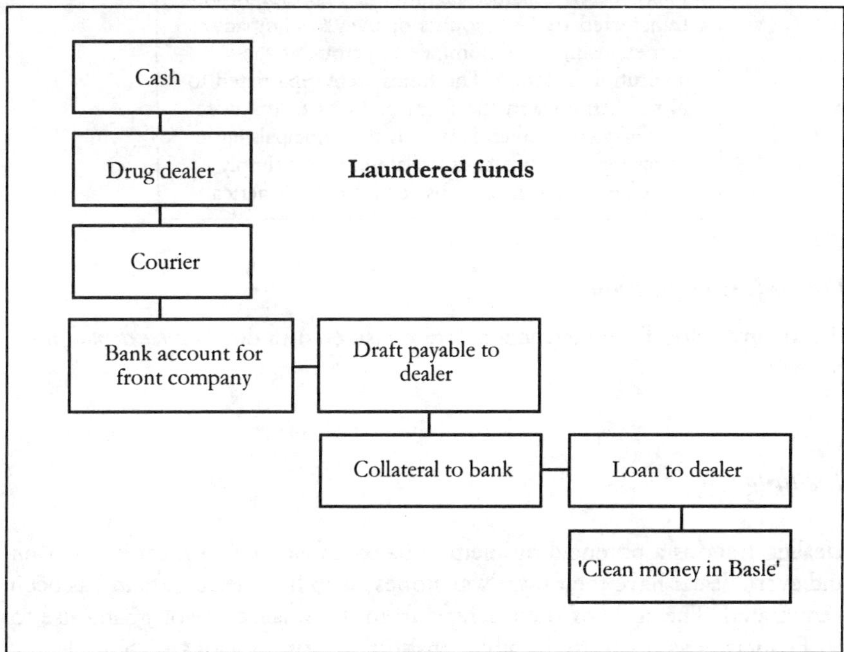

As the chart shows, cash received by a drug dealer is paid by a courier into an account in the name of a front company at a bank where an official is prepared to collude in money laundering. A draft is then issued and charged to the front company's account. The draft is used as collateral for a loan to the dealer which he never repays but which appears to be a legitimate explanation for funds received. As the launderer's expression goes, it has become 'clean money in Basle'.

Further examples of money laundering transactions are included in the digest of cases. Examples of suspicious transactions are also set out in the appendices. These examples are based on the guidance notes issued by the Joint Money Laundering Steering Group which should be consulted for further guidance.

> **Drugs money in disguise**
>
> Cash collected in the United States from street sales of drugs was smuggled across the border into Canada. The cash was changed for higher denomination notes at currency exchanges. Couriers then hand carried the cash by air to London where it was paid into a branch of a Jersey-based financial institution. The money was transferred to 14 accounts opened in company names, using local nominee directors, at the institution in Jersey. The funds were repatriated to North America in the form of loans to offshore property companies owned by the principals either using Jersey deposits as collateral or by simply transferring the money back to North America.

Fraudulent instructions

Frauds involving false instructions are considered under *Other external frauds* below.

Dealing

Dealing fraud is a potential problem in banks of all sizes. Almost every bank and every dealer have their own 'war stories' as to how dealing fraud has been perpetrated. The scale of fraud ranges from the small, perhaps giving rise to no financial loss, to those in which institutions lose millions of pounds.

A simple categorisation of dealing fraud would divide the frauds into two categories: misappropriation of funds, whereby a dealer takes funds from the institution, either directly or indirectly, for his own purpose; and false reporting or accounting, whereby a dealer ensures that the financial performance of the area under his control is misreported. This may or may not lead to a loss for the institution but in all cases would involve unauthorised activity. It may also result in a misleading impression being given of the financial soundness of the institution.

Motivation for dealing fraud includes:

- direct personal benefit – the dealer siphons off cash for his own use;
- job protection – the dealer incurs a loss and, in order to protect his position within the institution, seeks to hide the loss by the use of fraudulent transactions. In many cases the original loss may be due to a simple mistake or an error of judgement;
- to increase remuneration – this occurs indirectly by the use of some type of fraudulent transaction to inflate reported profits. In many institutions

dealers are remunerated both by means of a base salary and a performance-related bonus. The greater the profits shown in the particular dealer's book, the greater the performance bonus;
- protecting the future – this is the reverse of inflating profits, whereby, if a dealer has been particularly successful in one period, rather than recognising all the profit now he secretes an amount away to be released when trading is not so profitable.

In many cases the original motivation for dealing fraud is to protect a current position and not to defraud the institution of cash. Some of the more notable dealing frauds are 'downward spirals' whereby one unauthorised or fraudulent transaction leads to a complex web of transactions, which eventually give rise to a significant loss.

A typical sequence of events involves the dealer incurring, but not reporting, a loss (innocently or otherwise) or reporting a false profit. Having taken this initial step there is a need to generate profit to cover the loss or to realise the profit. In order to do this, the position is increased on the basis that, by taking a bigger position, the ability to make profit is increased. Having taken the bigger position, the market moves against that position such that the original loss becomes greater. The spiral then continues with the need to increase the position even further to be able to recover the loss. The spiral continues further until it becomes very complex, is hard to disguise and then is discovered.

As with lending and depositor frauds above, it is helpful to consider the various types of dealing fraud in the context of a typical dealing cycle. The dealing cycle may be broken down into the following key phases:

- dealer enters into the deal;
- a dealing slip or dealing sheet is completed;
- the deal is entered into the accounting system;
- the deal is matched with the counterparty;
- the deal is settled; and
- open positions are valued.

The second and third stages above may be simultaneous in certain computerised systems. The matching process may also be computerised.

In the first stage of the cycle the key concerns are the price at which the deal is struck and the dealer's relationship with the counterparty concerned. Typical frauds in this phase involve the use of false market prices, for example through off-market rings or related party deals. Concentration of business through particular brokers may indicate the existence of broker kickbacks, whereby the dealer receives a payment from a particular broker in return for passing business to the broker.

In the second and third phases of the cycle, completion of the deal slip and recording the deal in the accounting system, the main concern is that the deal is properly recorded and on a timely basis. Dealers may suppress deals to hide loss-making transactions or delay their input to keep within limits. Dealers may manipulate profits between client accounts and the firm's own portfolio. Dealers may also input fictitious transactions to avoid showing a loss, recognise a profit or disguise a position. Unnecessary suspense accounts should be closed as these are often used by fraudsters to cover their tracks.

As regards deal matching, opportunities for fraud may arise where deal matching procedures are weak or where there are known loopholes in computerised matching procedures. Possible frauds in the settlement phase are discussed later in this chapter under *Other banking frauds*. Some of the more general problems associated with the treasury area were discussed in the *Cash and payment systems* section of Chapter 4.

A key factor underlying many major dealing frauds is counterparties allowing deals to roll up without settlement. Certain contracts do not require immediate settlement, for example forward foreign exchange contracts and certain types of derivatives. There is a higher risk of fraud with instruments of this kind: there are cases of losses of hundreds of millions of pounds being accumulated and concealed.

Although individual losses may not be so great, the most common vulnerability is the misvaluation of positions. While many financial instruments have deep and liquid markets and market prices are freely available, the newer generation of financial products, particularly derivatives, pose significant valuation challenges. Overmarking a book may lead to bonuses being paid on false profits.

The above dealing frauds are summarised in the chart opposite:

Dealing cycle

Management and employee frauds

- Off-market rings
- Related party deals
- Broker kickbacks
- False deals

Dealer enters into deal

- Unrecorded deals
- Delayed deal allocations

Dealing slip is completed

- Misuse of discretionary accounts

Deal is recorded in the accounting system

- Exploiting weaknesses in matching procedures

Deal matched

- See *Other banking frauds*

Deal settled

- Mismarking of book
- Valuation rings

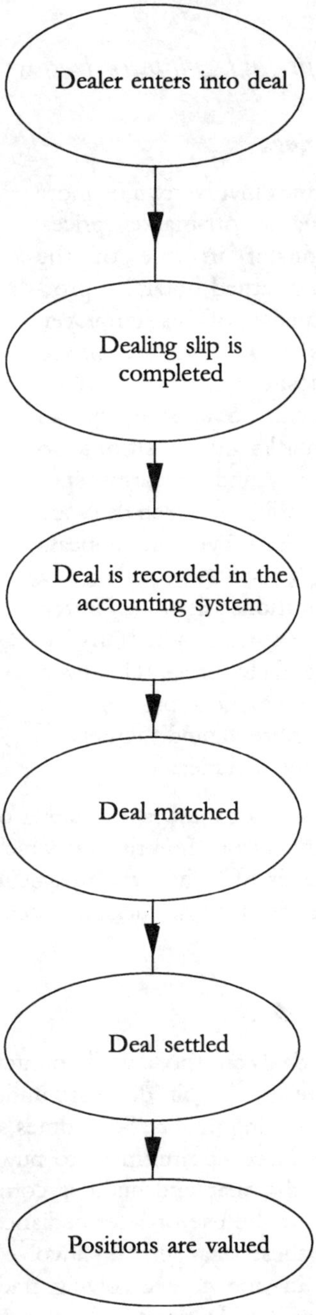

Positions are valued

Although the above frauds all appear to be management and employee frauds, in fact many may involve collusion with outsiders, in particular off-market rings, related party deals, broker kickbacks and valuation rings.

Management and employee frauds

Off-market rings

Off-market rings involve two or more parties dealing at off-market prices. Usually a dealer in one of the institutions concerned obtains a profit at the expense of his employer. However, as shown in the boxed example opposite, this type of fraud may be difficult to spot unless an institution marks its positions to market each day and performs spot checks on the prices at which deals are transacted, because everyone appears to be making a profit.

Most institutions in the United Kingdom mark their positions to market on a daily basis. However, there may be practical problems in doing this in more illiquid markets.

Warning signs include:

- dealing book not marked to market on a daily basis;
- no spot checks on the prices at which deals are transacted;
- unusual levels of activity with particular counterparties; and
- poor supervision in the dealing room.

Everyone seems to make a profit

A dealer at an institution bought a particular security at 100. He then sold the bond to an investor at 101, when the market price was 103, apparently making a profit of 1. The investor then sold the shares at 103 to another institution which in turn sold them on at a small profit to the first institution. Part of the profit made by the investor was paid as a kickback to the dealer at the first institution.

Related party deals

Related party deals are those with counterparties to whom the institution or the dealer is related. Again deals are undertaken at off-market prices with a view to manipulating profits. Sometimes securities are sold to related parties, with an undisclosed commitment to buy back the securities at a later date, perhaps after the year end audit is complete. These frauds often involve esoteric deals or the use of intermediaries, with no clear business purpose.

Sometimes these arrangements involve both related and unrelated parties. For example in one case involving trading in warrants the price of the warrants was artificially 'ramped' by a complex series of transactions between a number of institutions. In this type of fraud no loss is incurred until 'the music stops' and one of the unrelated parties is left holding virtually worthless stock. Usually this type of fraud succeeds because the unrelated parties in the ring do not fully understand the product.

Warning signs are as for *Off-market rings* above.

Broker kickbacks

A significant volume of transactions in the London markets are dealt through brokers rather than directly between counterparties. Brokers earn a commission on all transactions they arrange. In some cases commissions may be paid to the individual dealer as a form of kickback in order to increase the flow of deals through that broker. Such arrangements are difficult to identify.

Warning signs include:

- high levels of business with a particular broker; and
- unusual trends in broker commissions.

False deals

Dealers may input fictitious transactions into the system in order to avoid showing a loss, recognise a profit or disguise a position. Clearly the risk of false deals remaining undetected is increased significantly where deal matching procedures are weak.

Warning signs include:

- unusual trends in dealers' positions;
- significant number of unmatched or unconfirmed deals in particular dealing books or with particular counterparties;
- a significant number of cancelled deals; and
- unusually high value of unsettled transations.

Unrecorded deals

There may be a number of reasons why dealers want to delay inputting deals. For example, the dealer may wish to conceal loss making transactions or hide the fact that he has exceeded certain dealing limits (in many institutions exceeding limits is a dismissable offence).

Warning signs include:

- high levels of profit by particular dealers in relation to stated dealing strategy;
- dealing books trading close to their dealing limits;
- unusual trends in dealers' positions; and
- significant number of unmatched counterparty confirmations.

> ***No questions asked***
>
> A highly successful foreign exchange dealer, whose remuneration was linked closely to dealing profits earned, took unauthorised overnight positions in forward foreign exchange contracts. He booked the unauthorised deals the following day shortly before booking the deals which reversed the positions. Having made significant profits on one occasion the markets in New York and Tokyo moved against him overnight. He doubled up his positions assuming the market would continue in the same direction. However the market reversed. The unauthorised activity was not picked up because the back office focused almost exclusively on checking settlement details on incoming confirmations ignoring the trade dates and other details. Also details relative to forward deals were only checked as they reached settlement date. No questions were asked how the dealer managed to achieve a high level of profits despite a strategy where only very limited overnight positions were permitted.

Delayed deal allocation

In institutions which deal for their own account and for clients, dealers may deliberately delay the allocation of deals to clients or the institution, awaiting market movements. An example of this would be buying equities in the morning and then not allocating them to the client or the firm's own portfolio until the position has been sold later in the day such that profitable transactions are passed to an account set up by the dealer with loss making deals being booked to the client.

> ***Heads I win, tails I win***
>
> The head of foreign exchange at a bank helped an investor to earn 'profits' of approximately £0.5 million. Details of transactions were recorded on the dealer's trading sheet in pencil. Then the pencil entries were later overwritten in ink, putting in the known results instead of the speculated figures.

This type of fraud can operate in a number of ways with profitable deals being allocated to the institution itself or being targeted at particular clients who then reimburse the dealer for his efforts.

Warning signs include:

- no time stamping of deal tickets or a review of the time of booking;
- alterations to or overwriting of details on deal sheets; and
- abnormal profits or losses by particular dealers or certain of their clients.

Misuse of discretionary accounts

Discretionary dealing accounts, in the hands of experienced dealers, may provide an opportunity for secreting profits, hiding losses or generally manipulating results. While dealers will of course be accountable to the discretionary client, the dealer may use clever accounting devices and exploit timing differences to hide losses or manipulate results for the period he requires.

Warning signs include:

- unusual trends on particular discretionary accounts;
- sole contact clients;
- non-standard postings or adjustments to particular accounts; and
- special arrangements for preparation and issue of statements.

The risk of this type of fraud is increased where account statements are not despatched by personnel independent of the dealing room. Also in many systems the quality of reporting in relation to client accounts is inferior to the bank's own trading. Poor quality statements can sometimes conceal the nature and extent of a client's exposure. Also, many clients do not check their statements very closely, particularly if they appear to be making profits. As with *Unrecorded deals* above, it is essential to question abnormal levels of profit achieved by individual dealers in relation to particular client accounts against the agreed dealing strategy.

Exploiting weaknesses in deal matching procedures

Rigorous deal matching procedures are crucial in any dealing system. All deal details should be agreed with the counterparty as soon as possible. Where such procedures are weak or where there are loopholes in computerised deal matching programs, opportunities for fraud may occur.

It is difficult to identify warning signs for this particular type of fraud. Once programmed, it is likely that staff will place unquestioning reliance on a computer matching process. The problem may therefore go undetected for a considerable period.

A loophole in the programme

In an FX dealing operation the computer would only process transactions where all specified fields matched with the counterparty's details. However, due to a computer programming error the computer did not compare trade date details. The loophole allowed certain dealers to misrepresent their positions by recording them on other than their actual trade dates.

Mismarking the book

One of the more difficult areas in a dealing portfolio is determining market values for reporting purposes at the end of reporting periods. For certain financial instruments quoted prices are available which can be determined and checked with a reasonable amount of accuracy. In other instruments, markets are thinner or pricing arrangements are complex such that there is considerable scope for dealers to over or under value positions in order to achieve their target level of performance.

The tremendous growth in over-the-counter products, particularly derivatives, and the way in which the markets in such products are becoming increasingly complex, provides significant scope for misvaluation. Institutions most susceptible to this type of fraud are those where the gap between the experience, knowledge and ability of front office personnel and that of back office personnel, financial control and general management is greatest.

In many of the newer products there is no market price and on a large book, a misvaluation by only a few points can have a significant impact on reported profits. Within any institution which has a significant amount of over-the-counter and derivative products, thorough independent review and testing of prices used for profit reporting is an essential financial control.

Warning signs of position misvaluation include:

- no detailed valuation policies and guidelines; and
- unusual trends in the value of particular books.

> ***The markets didn't obey me . . .***
>
> An interest rate options dealer at a bank manipulated revaluation rates to hide an unrealised loss of £3 million, because the market had moved against him. Trading in interest rate options had commenced at the bank before back-office procedures were fully in place. In particular there was no facility for the back-office to check the valuation of interest rate options independently.

Valuation rings

Position values are often checked by comparing revaluation prices to third party sources. In certain cases however the dealer at the institution may have agreed with the third party that in a response to a request for information they should provide non-market prices.

OTHER BANKING FRAUDS

In this section we examine certain other fraudulent techniques used in banks. Most of these techniques occur in a wide range of banking situations.

> ***Management and employee frauds***
>
> - Omitted contingencies
> - Passing through (*concealment device*)
> - Rolling matching (*concealment device*)
> - Diverted postings (*concealment device*)
> - Misuse of volume accounts (*concealment device*)

Management and employee frauds

Omitted contingencies

Omitted contingency frauds involve the giving of unrecorded guarantees or other commitments. There is no immediate movement of funds making these frauds easier to conceal. Quite often such undisclosed guarantees and commitments are connected with some other kind of transaction, such as the transfer of a problem loan to another part of the group or an associate.

Warning signs include:

- evidence of guarantee fees or telex messages to counterparties with whom the bank does not normally deal; and
- documentation kept in management offices to which access is restricted.

> ***Side deal***
>
> The chairman of a bank gave a guarantee to a customer of a bank overseas of which he was also a director. The management of the bank was unaware that the guarantee had been given.

The risk of this type of fraud may be increased where there are weak controls over the giving and recording of guarantees and other commitments.

Passing through

As already explained, passing through involves paying away receipts without recording the receipt or the repayment in the accounting records, usually to enable benefits to be paid direct to directors or employees.

Warning signs include a large number of contra items on nostro reconciliations.

Sole customer contacts increase the risk of this type of fraud.

Rolling matching

As explained in the previous chapter, rolling matching is the incorrect matching of items on reconciliations to facilitate the concealment of fraudulent items. Rolling matching is most likely to happen when numerous items of a similar amount flow through an account. The reconciliation may appear to work. However, full reperformance of the reconciliation will reveal that the reconciling items are not those shown but other items which appear to have been matched.

The risk of this type of fraud is increased where there is no periodic reperformance of reconciliations. Cursory review of reconciliations by management is insufficient. Excessive numbers of contras and journals may be a warning sign.

Diverted postings

Diverted postings may be used in virtually any area of a bank. For example, a bank may enter into transactions so that a customer is able to obtain some benefit, often illegally, such as export credits, grants or a tax benefit. In return the customer may agree for his account to be used in an irregular manner by the bank. For example, loans may be concealed by debiting them to the account of such a customer and providing the customer with documentation to 'hold him harmless' for the loan.

Warning signs include:

- unusual terms or activity on particular accounts; and
- any evidence that a bank is actively involved in helping persons in other jurisdictions to break local laws.

Misuse of volume accounts

Where large numbers of transactions flow through a particular account, this may enable the fraudster to conceal fraudulent transactions more easily. For example, the fraudster may charge relatively small amounts regularly to interest expense accounts, crediting the equivalent amount to his own or his nominee's account. It may be difficult to detect this type of fraud because exact amounts may be charged so that the correlation between interest expense and deposit liabilities is maintained. Similar types of manipulation may happen in other areas of a bank's operations.

Warning signs include:

- terms of business which are unusual; and
- journals and adjustments posted to volume accounts which are not adequately explained.

The risk of this type of fraud is increased where there is no independent review of personal accounts and no independent review of interest rates charged or credited on particular accounts.

External frauds

- Cross firing (or 'cheque kiting')
- Cheque frauds/new account frauds
- Misuse of money transfer systems
- Advance fee fraud
- Credit card fraud

Cross firing (or 'cheque kiting')

Cross firing involves the accumulation of balances on bank accounts based on uncollected cheques drawn on accounts at other banks. The fraudster takes advantage of the timing delays inherent in the banking system to increase, artificially, his reserves or reduce his cost of funding. Often a multiplicity of accounts is used. Most banks are alert to this type of fraud.

Warning signs include:

- many deposits of similar and/or round sum amounts;
- a high proportion of transactions regularly with another bank;
- deposits soon withdrawn;
- flow through account does not seem to have a business reason; and
- accounts with low average balance but a high volume of transactions.

Cheque frauds/new account frauds

As with *Cross firing*, most banks have taken steps to deal with this type of fraud. The fraudster's techniques include impersonation, giving false details, altering payee details, forging signatures and manufacturing copies of company cheques. Sometimes the photocopies are so good that only forensic tests distinguish them from the real thing.

Warning signs include:

- alterations to cheques;
- illegible signatures;

> ***219 false bank accounts***
>
> Two individuals opened 219 accounts at banks across the country using addresses from voters' registers then getting the Post Office to redirect the mail to an accommodation address in Slough on the pretext of moving house.

- inconsistencies in printing;
- customers resident outside the normal trading area of the branch or bank;
- undue haste to open accounts;
- unusual behaviour of the applicant; and
- inconsistencies arising from credit status and other checks.

Misuse of money transfer systems

Some of the largest frauds, or attempted frauds, have involved the misuse of money transfer systems. The fraudster may attempt to transfer funds, securities or other assets. Fortunately many of the attempts are not successful. However, reported cases are relatively common and many attempted frauds are never reported. Many of the attempts are only discovered by chance rather than any particular strength in the banks' preventive controls.

> ***Unauthorised use of SWIFT codes***
>
> Six people allegedly attempted to defraud a bank. It was alleged that the money was transferred after correct codes and procedures authorising the transaction were received by the bank overseas. The fraud attempts were not made by hacking into the bank's computer. The fraud was discovered by accident during a manual check of transactions after a computer breakdown.

Warning signs include:

- control over final release of funds insufficient for the amounts involved – e.g., checking only that the signatory is authorised to sign;
- transfers to or from accounts in offshore locations or countries with bank secrecy laws;
- transfers to or from individuals who are not regular customers;
- abbreviated payee names or instructions and alterations to the date, amount, payee or other details;
- poor control of documents between approval and processing;
- processing of significant transactions by junior personnel; and
- poor security over the room where transfers are made or over codes and passwords.

Advance fee fraud

Advance fee fraud was discussed in the previous chapter. This type of fraud also occurs in the financial sector and often involves complex transactions and documents. For example, in one case a lawyer claimed that he represented an overseas financial services firm. He took fees to secure loans on favourable terms. The loans never materialised.

Possible warning signs are as set out under *Advance fee fraud* in the previous chapter.

Credit card fraud

Credit card fraud is a major problem for all of the credit card companies. Typical frauds include forged cards, theft of credit cards and misuse of credit card details. Detailed consideration of credit card fraud is outside the scope of this guide.

Investment business

In this section we look at some of the most common frauds in client investment business.

Investment business

Management and employee frauds
- Bogus investments
- Trading without authorisation
- Selling client investments without authority
- Dealing room fraud
- Share ramping
- Insider dealing
- Churning
- Other management and employee frauds

External frauds
- Money laundering
- Bogus documents/stolen share certificates
- Fraudulent instructions

A number of the above frauds are similar to frauds discussed elsewhere in this guide. For example, the frauds involving bogus investments are similar to the frauds involving bogus goods or services discussed under *Sales* in Chapter 4. All of these frauds involve the sale of products which are 'too good to be true', marketed in a convincing way to a vulnerable customer base. They usually involve a complex web of deceit including false accounting records and bogus documentation. The businesses are often seemingly very successful, having achieved extraordinary growth.

Selling clients investments without authority overlaps with certain of the depositor frauds discussed earlier in this chapter. Dealing room fraud has been discussed in a banking context. Most of these frauds are equally prevalent in investment business. Share ramping and insider dealing have also been discussed earlier. These frauds may be perpetrated by anyone who has access to inside information: officers of the company, dealers in the companies' shares, merchant bankers and other advisers. Money laundering has also been discussed in the context of non financial sector businesses and in banks. In this section we discuss briefly some of the specific concerns in investment business.

Management and employee frauds

Bogus investments

As noted in Chapter 4, bogus product frauds have been particularly prevalent in the financial sector in recent years. Typically private investors invest savings in seemingly low risk, high return products. The products may be attractively 'packaged' and the fraudster goes to a lot of trouble to make sure all the 'right' documentation is in place.

However, the funds are either invested in highly speculative investments on which the fraudster hopes to make secret profits or the funds are diverted for his personal use.

> ***A paper chase***
>
> A commodity company gave the impression that it invested clients' funds properly. In fact the funds were not invested in commodities at all but in the fraudsters' own bank accounts. The fraudsters generated false internal documentation, accounting records and statements for clients. They also arranged bogus 'third-party' confirmations for the auditors.

Sometimes investors are induced to invest in bogus shares of a speculative nature or offering some inducement. For example, in one case people were deceived into believing that investing in a particular company's shares would exempt them from the poll tax. In another case it was claimed that the company was developing a miracle way of detecting salmonella and listeria bacteria.

Warning signs include:

- products 'too good to be true' – for example, low risk, high return products;
- glossy advertising/high pressure sales techniques targetted at a vulnerable and inexperienced client base (for example, the elderly, the unemployed or inexperienced investors);

> ***An anagram for offshore***
>
> The director of an investment company induced people to invest money in high return offshore trusts. He actually spent their money on a system of horse-race betting. Investors inquiring about their money were told it was 'offshore' – a mixture according to the fraudster of 'off' and an anagram of 'horse' . . .

- explanation of transaction is complex or investments are in companies based on one-off ventures or promoting some 'miracle' product;
- abnormal levels of growth in profitability or margins achieved;
- documentation held in the offices of senior officers of the company which it is claimed have no connection with the business; and
- complex accounting arrangements over use of intermediaries, companies in offshore locations or other factors which make it difficult to trace the movement of funds or investments.

Trading without authorisation

There has been a number of reported cases of individuals attempting to carry on investment business without having received authorisation from the appropriate regulatory authority to carry on such business. While it will be clear whether or not authorisation has been obtained, it may be less clear whether further authorisation is required for new business areas.

> ***Clients' money used to fund stock market losses***
>
> Two individuals used over £100,000 of clients' money to fund personal losses made on the stock market. The individuals had failed to provide proper details to the regulator to allow them to be authorised under the Financial Services Act 1986 but had continued to tell clients that they were authorised.

Perhaps more common, although often unreported, are businesses which submit false or misleading information to the regulator. Examples include misdescription of assets or omission of liabilities to inflate the net worth of the company to continue to meet capital adequacy requirements.

Warning signs include:

- new business developments where detailed advice has not been sought concerning the regulatory implications;
- tight liquidity position;
- unusual trends; and
- transactions with suspected related parties.

Selling or lending client investments without authority

This type of fraud includes selling shares or other securities on behalf of clients without their authority, or surrendering client endowment policies and single premium bonds and investment bonds without their consent. Alternatively, client securities could be used as collateral to secure the liabilities of the fraudster, perhaps represented as having been 'stock lent' by the client.

Warning signs include:

- abnormal level of client sales or policy surrenders given stated investment strategy or unexpected departures from agreed investment strategy;
- evidence of significant personal dealing; and
- missing documentation or authority letters or unusual aspects on client files.

> ***Investment adviser cashes in client policies***
>
> An investment adviser sold clients' endowment policies, single premium bonds and investment bonds. His clients were mainly retired people of modest means. He forged clients' signatures and surrendered policies without their consent in an attempt to recoup stock market losses amounting to £1.6 million incurred during 1987.

Dealing fraud

Dealing frauds were discussed in the banking section above. All of these frauds are equally prevalent in an investment business context.

Share ramping

We discussed share ramping and other similar schemes in Chapter 4 (see *Other frauds*) and in the section on dealing frauds earlier in this chapter. Share ramping involves financial advisers, company executives or others buying substantial amounts of a company's shares at inflated prices to give a false impression of their value.

Warning signs include:

- abnormal increases in the prices of shares of companies for which the company acts as adviser or sponsor;
- loans or transactions, the commercial purpose of which is unclear; and

> ***The Panamanian bubble***
>
> The MD of a financial services company, who acted as financial adviser to a number of small quoted companies, used a Panamanian company to buy on credit four million of the seven million shares available in a particular company at inflated prices, thus giving a false impression of their value.

- complex structures/transactions with offshore or 'front' companies.

Front running

Dealers may make profits on their own account by personally entering into deals ahead of transactions to be made by the fund they manage. This type of fraud may be difficult to detect unless detailed analysis of transactions is undertaken. Clearly the absence of strict rules on and monitoring of own account dealings increases the risk of this type of fraud.

Insider dealing

> ***Making a quick buck***
>
> A management consultant who had been asked by an insurance company to devise an incentive scheme to ensure that senior executives of a company which it was due to purchase would stay on after the takeover bought shares in the target company shortly afterwards and sold them on at a 50 per cent profit three weeks later.

We discussed insider dealing in Chapter 4, for example where the directors of a company may deal in the company's shares prior to the announcement of worse than expected results or before the announcement of a takeover bid.

As illustrated in the example opposite financial advisers to a company or consultants may also obtain unpublished price sensitive information and be tempted to make a quick profit.

For warning signs see *Other frauds* in Chapter 4.

Churning

Churning involves the excessive buying and selling of securities for the main purpose of generating commission. This usually occurs where a broker is acting in a discretionary capacity or as investment manager for a particular client.

Warning signs include:

- unusually high levels of activity on particular clients or high commission levels for particular clients or brokers;
- apparent departures from agreed investment strategy; and
- client rarely in contact with the broker – for example, abroad for long periods.

Other management and employee frauds

Other employee frauds in investment business include misuse of cheques, dealers using false client names on dealing slips and contract notes, theft of share certificates and misuse of discretionary powers.

> ***Back office fraud***
>
> An employee in an investment business presented cheques for signature purporting to be payments of investment sale proceeds to clients. The payee was always a bank. The employee subsequently added his own bank account number to the payee names.

External frauds

Money laundering

We have already discussed money laundering in connection with the manufacturing and service sectors and banking business. Investment business is also vulnerable to money laundering.

Cash settlement of investment transactions is sufficiently rare in the United Kingdom to attract immediate attention. Therefore investment businesses are less likely than banks and building societies to be at risk during the initial placement stage. However, bearer securities delivered other than through an established clearing system should merit special attention.

Investment businesses are more likely to find themselves being used at the layering and integration stages. The liquidity of many investment products particularly attracts sophisticated money launderers since it allows them quickly and easily to move the money from one product to another, mixing lawful and illicit proceeds.

Although long-standing customers may launder money through an investment business, it is more likely to be a new customer who may use one or more accounts for a short period only and may use false names and fictitious companies. Investment may be direct with a United Kingdom investment business or indirect via an intermediary who 'doesn't ask too many awkward questions'. This is a particular risk in jurisdictions where money laundering is not legislated against or where the rules are not vigorously enforced. Intermediaries increase opacity and, depending on the designation of the account, may preserve anonymity. Numbered accounts may also be used to delay, obscure or avoid detection.

Examples of unusual dealing patterns and abnormal transactions include:

- a large number of security transactions across a number of jurisdictions;
- transactions not in keeping with the investor's normal activity, financial markets in which the investor is active and the business which the investor operates;
- buying and selling of securities with no discernible purpose or in circumstances which appear unusual – churning at the client's request;
- low grade securities purchased in an overseas jurisdiction, sold in the United Kingdom and high grade securities purchased with the proceeds;
- bearer securities held outside a recognised custodial system;
- a number of transactions by the same counterparty in small amounts of

the same security, each purchased for cash and then sold in one transaction, the proceeds being credited to an account different from the original account;

- early termination of packaged products at a loss due to front end loading: early cancellation, especially where cash has been tendered and/or the refund cheque is to a third party;
- transfer of investments to apparently unrelated third parties;
- transactions not in keeping with normal practice in the market to which they relate, for example with reference to market size and frequency or at off-market prices; and
- other transactions linked to the transaction in question which could be designed to disguise money and divert it into other forms or other destinations or beneficiaries.

Unusual settlement activity might include large transaction settlements by cash or settlement by way of third-party cheque or money transfer where there is variation between the account holder, signatory and the prospective investor.

Other unusual circumstances would include:

- payments to a third party without any apparent connection with the investor; and
- settlement either by registration or delivery of securities to be made to an unverified third party.

Bogus documents/stolen share certificates

Most investment businesses take good care of share certificates, bearer documents and other valuable assets in their custody. Nevertheless, frauds in this area are surprisingly common.

Warning signs include:

- weaknesses in physical security procedures;
- overdue reconciliations of custody records to securities held on the premises or to other depositaries;
- significant number of items on reconciliations which cannot be explained; and
- insufficient resources or inexperienced staff allocated to safe custody activities.

> **_Stolen share certificates_**
>
> Three individuals defrauded banks, stockbrokers and financial institutions of £12.5 million by inducing them to accept share certificates which had been stolen from a major securities house. They tried to sell them through other brokers and to raise loans using the stolen share as security.

Fraudulent instructions

Fraudulent instructions may include forged signatures on share transfer forms, forged power of attorney, bogus fax messages or unauthorised use of codes and passwords to transfer securities electronically.

Warning signs include:

- instructions out of line with clients' usual activities;
- abnormal haste to complete the transaction; and
- unusual aspects in documentation, for example small differences in letterheads, paper used, type script, handwriting or postmarks.

The risk of this type of fraud is increased where significant transactions are undertaken without contacting the customer directly or where there is poor security over codes and passwords.

> ***Forged power of attorney***
>
> Two individuals allegedly plotted to obtain shares from a bank. The bank held the shares on behalf of one of the individual's great aunt. He had flown to his great aunt's villa abroad and obtained a specimen signature. A letter was then allegedly forged saying that he had power of attorney for her. The letter was used in an attempt to obtain the shares.

Insurance

As with investment business, a number of the frauds discussed in this section are similar to frauds discussed elsewhere in this guide. For example, persuading customers to cancel policies against their interests, forged surrender of policies or claims and misappropriation of funds invested are similar to certain of the banking and investment business frauds discussed above. Some of the frauds involving false insurance claims are similar in certain respects to the external purchasing frauds discussed in Chapter 4. However, as before, it is useful to look at these frauds in the context of insurance business to understand the nature of the threat.

Insurance

Management and employee frauds
- Bogus policies
- Persuading customers to cancel policies against their interests
- Forged surrender of policies
- Misappropriation of funds invested

External frauds
- False statements/failure to disclose relevant information
- Bogus policy holders
- Staged deaths/accidents/thefts/arson frauds
- Inflated/false/composite claims
- Money laundering

Management and employee frauds

Bogus policies

These frauds include producing bogus insurance products, such as capital investment bonds, bogus cover notes and insurance policies and the manipulation of risk classes by agents.

Non-existent insurance company

Four individuals collected premiums on commercial liability policies, performance bonds and financial guarantees for building contractors. They issued policies through an insurance agent in which one of them was an officer, in the name of a non-existent insurance company apparently incorporated in Anguilla. They provided potential policy holders and agents with false financial statements which showed that the insurance company had substantial assets to meet claims.

Persuading customers to cancel policies against their interests

This type of fraud enables insurance companies or their agents to generate commissions fraudulently by persuading customers to cancel existing policies against their interests and take out new ones.

Warning signs include:

Too good to be true

An insurance agent induced policy holders to take out new policies, giving them misleading information about interest rates and dividends. However, instead of terminating the old policies he took out loans on them, only later terminating the old policies and rolling them over into new ones.

- abnormal level of early policy surrenders; and
- unusual trends in commission levels.

Forged surrender of policies/claims

> **Forged signatures**
>
> A life insurance agent identified policy holders who had ceased to pay premiums. He then forged the policy holders' signatures on policy surrender documents and sent them to head office requesting that the cheques be sent back to him for delivery. He forged endorsements and banked the cheques.

Forged surrender of policies often occur where customers' policies have become dormant. The agent forges surrender documentation and pockets the surrender proceeds himself.

Misappropriation of funds

Misappropriation of funds can occur in a large number of situations: for example, diverting funds handed over by investors for investment in policies, or insurance company employees submitting fictitious claims relating to non-existent dependents of eligible policy holders.

Warning signs include:

- unusual trends in commissions earned by particular salesmen;
- no independent spot checking of information on claim forms; and
- customer complaints/general correspondence not monitored independently.

> **Defrauding investors**
>
> A life insurance salesman defrauded 400 investors of their life savings. The salesman accepted funds for investment in policies. He arranged for a monthly income to be paid to the investors, misappropriating the larger part of the funds invested. The insurance company did not admit legal responsibility but paid substantial compensation to the victims of the fraud.

External frauds

False statements/failure to disclose relevant information

False statements and failure to disclose relevant information covers a very wide range of matters, such as age, state of health, previous convictions, financial details and other insurances held. Most insurance companies are alert to the risks in this area.

Bogus policy holders

Bogus policy holder frauds usually involve impersonation and/or submission of false information.

Warning signs include:

Men of straw

An individual who ran his own accountancy practice allegedly defrauded insurance companies of £1.9 million in respect of pension schemes set up for bogus companies. He set up an advisory insurance company to help clients in his accountancy practice. In the course of his accountancy business his clients gave him details of themselves and their families. It was alleged that he later used these details when putting forward forged documents to insurance companies. It was also alleged that he set up bogus companies and attributed to them bogus employees. He then took out pension schemes for these bogus businesses. In return he received large sums of money by way of insurance commission.

- common or like-sounding names between various policy holders;
- no spot checks on information on application forms;
- unusual trends in payment of premiums; and
- incomplete or scrappy documentation accompanying applications.

Staged deaths/accidents/thefts/arson frauds

This type of fraud is a major threat to all insurance companies. Cases include false claims on life policies, bogus accident claims, arson or otherwise destroying the insured assets and false claims by insurance company employees based on customer policies.

Most insurance companies are alert to the risks in this area. Certain insurance companies now use databases which enable multiple claims for the same loss, claimants' financial commitments, records of County Court judgments and anomalies in name and addresses to be identified.

Warning signs will depend on the particular circumstances. These frauds are often only uncovered by detailed appraisal of claims to ascertain all the facts relating to the claim.

Inflated/false/composite claims

Inflated/false/composite claims can again occur in a very wide range of situations. Once again most insurance companies are alert to the risks in this area and make use of sophisticated databases and cross-checks to identify fraudulent claims.

The dividing line between an optimistic assessment of loss (especially business interruption) and fraud is a grey area. For example, in many business interruption claims it will so happen that the period in which the event of the claim occurred would have been the best period ever. However, in some claims the claimant may make false representations, for example regarding orders received.

Money laundering

It may not appear immediately obvious how insurance products might be used for money laundering purposes. At the initial placement stage intermediate and product providers who deal directly with the public are the most vulnerable if they receive cash. However, retail investment products are more likely to be used at the layering and integration stages. For example, the liquidity of a unit trust may attract money launderers since it allows them quickly and easily to move their money from one product to another, mixing lawful and illicit proceeds and integrating them into the legitimate economy.

Lump sum investments in liquid products are clearly most vulnerable to use by money launderers, particularly where they are of high value. Payment in cash is likely to need further investigation, particularly where it cannot be supported by evidence of a cash-based business as the source of the funds.

> ***Early surrender***
>
> Money from drug trafficking was deposited into a number of United Kingdom bank accounts and then transferred to an offshore account. The trafficker entered into a £50,000 life insurance contract, having been introduced by a broking firm. Payment was made by two separate transfers from the offshore account. The funds were represented as the proceeds of overseas investments. At the time of the trafficker's arrest the insurer had received instructions for the early surrender of the contract.

Other frauds in the financial sector

In the final part of this chapter we deal with frauds in mortgage lending and leasing. These frauds are similar to certain of the lending frauds discussed at the beginning of this chapter.

> *Other frauds in the financial sector*
>
> *Mortgage lending*
> - Fictitious borrowers/false information on mortgage applications
>
> *Leasing*
> - Bogus HP agreements/leases for non-existent equipment

Mortgage lending

Fictitious borrowers/false information on mortgage applications

During the 1980's building societies and banks were defrauded of considerable sums of money in connection with their mortgage lending activities. In a time of rising prices and significant changes in the financial services industry, building societies and banks sought to gain market share. Unfortunately lending criteria were often poor, or were poorly applied. Opportunities for the fraudster were considerable.

Market conditions have changed considerably since that time and most building societies and banks have tightened up their procedures. However, this type of fraud remains a threat and if market conditions were to change the risk of mortgage fraud would increase also.

Frauds involving false or incomplete information are closely linked to fictitious borrower frauds. The individual making the application may be the person named on the form but some or all of the other details may be false: for example, false employment details, employment references, tenancy details and references or bogus valuations.

Many mortgage frauds involve collusion with valuers and solicitors and the double-pledging of collateral.

Warning signs are as for *Loans to fictitious borrowers* and *Impersonation/false information on loan applications* under *Lending* above.

128 false applications on more than 90 properties

A group of 19 people, including solicitors, valuers and property developers, made 128 applications for mortgages on more than 90 properties. The applications, which included false valuations by valuers, were made by the property developers who often used fictitious names. Certain solicitors also colluded in the frauds.

Family of seven make 54 false mortgage applications

Members of a family allegedly made 54 fraudulent mortgage applications, amounting to £1 million, over a period of eight years. Many mortgages were allegedly obtained by submitting details of fictitious employments, fictitious landlords and false employment references. 19 properties were used more than once as collateral in the applications.

Leasing

Bogus hire purchase agreements/non-existent equipment

Leasing frauds usually involve leases for non-existent equipment or vehicles. Frauds have included submitting signed documentation to companies from customers who had in fact changed their mind and decided to pay the car dealer cash: the dealer therefore gets paid twice for the same car. Similarly leasing companies have 'double dipped' into bank finance of their lease portfolios by writing fictitious leases.

Other frauds have involved equipment manufacturers forging the signatures of customers entering into leases with leading finance houses for non-existent computer equipment or lessees giving false acceptance certificates and using the finance for some other purpose.

> ***Leases on registration numbers***
>
> A car dealer used unused registration numbers for new cars to obtain cash from hire purchase companies. He then sold the same car with a real registration number to a genuine customer, thereby getting paid twice.

Warning signs include:

- no physical inspection of the leased asset;
- abnormal levels of business via particular agents; and
- inconsistencies in lease documentation.

Conclusion

The risk of fraud in financial sector businesses is considerable owing to the complexity of the business and the speed of transactions. Understandably companies in the financial sector focus on these more specialised risks. However, as noted in the introduction to this guide, it is important not to overlook the more general types of fraud which may affect any company. Most of the large businesses in the financial sector for example, have significant procurement spends. Procurement fraud and certain of the other frauds discussed in Chapter 4 are just as much an issue for these companies as they are for companies in the manufacturing or services sector.

6 Computer risks

Introduction

In the 1960's and 1970's, so called 'computer fraud' was talked about with much speculation but little evidence that computers posed any serious added threats, as regards fraud at least. The first major fraud which appeared to fall into the category of computer fraud was The Equity Funding Corporation case in 1973. The shares of The Equity Funding Corporation of America were suspended on the New York Stock Exchange in March of that year and investigations revealed a massive fraud aimed at maintaining the company's trading record and share price. Although heralded at the time as a computer-related fraud, this was only true to the extent that a computer system was used during the insurance phase of the fraud. A large number of fictitious insurance policies was created generating an estimated $29 million in bogus income in the last four years of a fraud involving some $146 million over ten years.

We noted in the introduction to this guide that most so-called computer frauds are not computer frauds at all: the computer is merely the medium through which transactions are processed. However, there are areas in which frauds may be perpetrated for which computers and high speed communications networks provide the essential ingredients to the fraud. Examples of this include program fraud and frauds relying on the speed of international payment systems for their effectiveness.

Since the Equity Funding case many new forms of fraud and abuse have emerged as technology has developed and computer literacy has increased. As more computers moved to on-line processing and telecommunications improved, computer hackers became a threat. Similarly, as the popularity of personal computers increased, viruses emerged as a significant problem and prevention of software theft became more difficult. Technological change continues, every new innovation potentially increasing the risk of fraud or abuse. Particular problems include:

- organisations becoming more and more dependent on their systems for operational as well as accounting and management information systems;
- open systems and networks which bring added risks of hacking and illegal access;
- systems integration which is pulling down the ring fences around different computer applications, improving efficiency, but increasing the

potential impact of any problems and the importance of good controls over access;

- the continuing shift from centralised mainframe computers to small networks under the control of end-users, who often have little understanding of the threats and necessary counter measures, which has increased many organisations' exposure to fraud; and
- the increasing complexity of technology which makes it more difficult to check that all major loopholes in controls are closed.

Automation often results in fewer people understanding how a process actually works – the system is seen as a 'black box'. This makes it more difficult for management to understand the risks and to design and implement effective controls. The need for tight physical control over cash is obvious and decisions about how to provide that control are relatively easy to make. However, the risks in computerised systems are much more difficult to identify and deciding what controls to use and where they should be placed is a complex challenge. This problem is often compounded by poor communication between the managers responsible for internal controls, frequently accountants by training, and technical computer specialists. In addition, the imposition of controls over systems may conflict with easy access and flexibility making the safeguards difficult to justify.

There are few reasons to retain clerically intensive, paper-based procedures. Technology can be used to reduce risks in ways that were not possible in manual systems where the information is hidden in paper files. Computers make it much easier to scan for potentially fraudulent transactions. Sophisticated 'expert systems' are being used to spot potentially fraudulent credit card transactions as they occur. Regulatory organisations are electronically monitoring financial trading as it happens and analysing trends to identify breaches of rules and possible cases of insider trading.

Computers can be both friend and foe. The key is to understand the risks associated with the systems and adopt a structured approach to controlling them.

The extent of computer fraud and abuse

Based on available information, computer fraud is a real threat, but its extent, like all fraud, is difficult to assess.

The most authoritative United Kingdom survey on computer fraud is conducted every three years by the Audit Commission. They cover computer fraud and abuse from a broad section of the private and public sector. There were 1,000 responses to the 1993 survey.

There are four main areas of computer fraud and abuse identified in the surveys:

Fraud	***Theft***	***Hacking***	***Virus***
Unauthorised alteration of input	of data	Deliberately gaining unauthorised access to a system through the use of communication facilities	Distributing a program with the intention of corrupting a computer process
Destruction, suppression or misappropriation of output from a computer process or equipment	of software	sabotaging the computer process by causing deliberate damage to the processing cycle	
Alteration of computerised data	using illicit copies of software		
Alteration or misuse of programs, excluding viruses	using computers for unauthorised private work		

Analysis of reported incidents

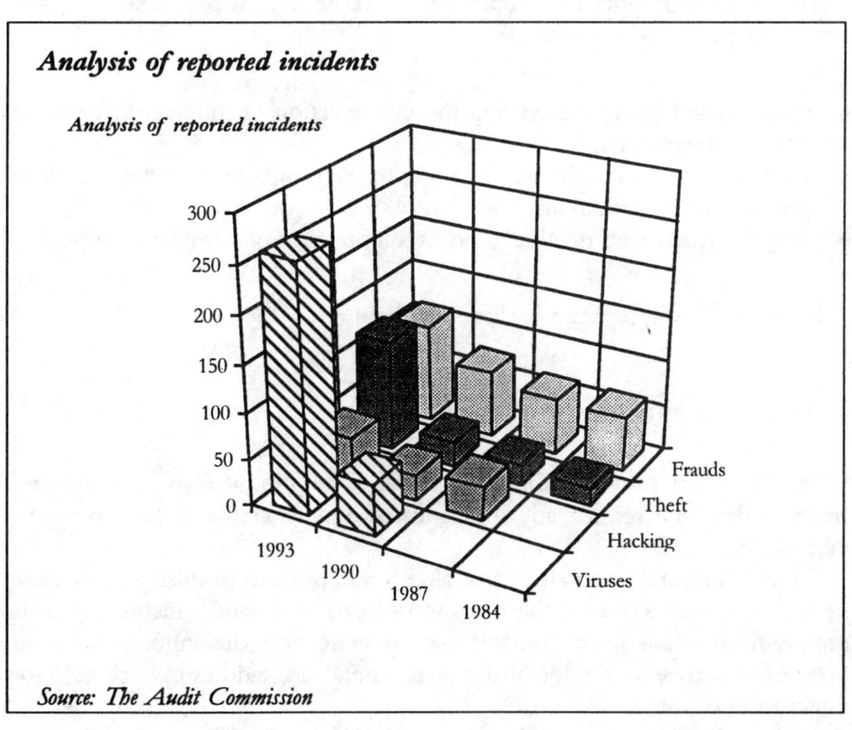

Source: The Audit Commission

The breakdown of reported computer frauds indicated that approximately half of the reported frauds were in fact related to the unauthorised alteration of input. Only 5.5 per cent of reported cases (less than one per cent by value of losses) were classified as being related to the alteration or misuse of computer programs.

The most alarming finding of the survey was the fact that half of reported computer frauds (52 per cent) were discovered accidentally. Only 39 per cent of frauds were uncovered by internal controls and 9 per cent by auditors. This suggests that few internal control systems in place were effective for computer fraud detection, although their deterrent effect is difficult to assess.

How does computer fraud occur?

The easiest way to understand how computer fraud occurs is to look at the typical path of transactions through a system.

The diagram opposite gives a simplified overview of the main processes which occur in a typical computer system. The type and amount of equipment will vary enormously from one company to another, as will the way it is linked together, but the processes are consistent.

The three main types of computer fraud relate directly to the key stages in computer processing. These are:

- input-related (usually involving the manipulation of the data to be input into the computer);
- system-related (unauthorised changes to the programs or systems used to process the information); and
- output-related (the manipulation or suppression of computer output).

Each of these categories is discussed below.

INPUT-RELATED COMPUTER FRAUD

Input fraud is the most common and easiest to commit form of computer fraud. It does not require any sophisticated understanding of technology to perpetrate.

Where it is possible to amend or alter input, prior to or during its capture by the computer systems, there is the potential for fraud. Accordingly it is important that adequate controls should exist over the input sources to prevent or detect the unauthorised alteration, addition, deletion or duplication of input.

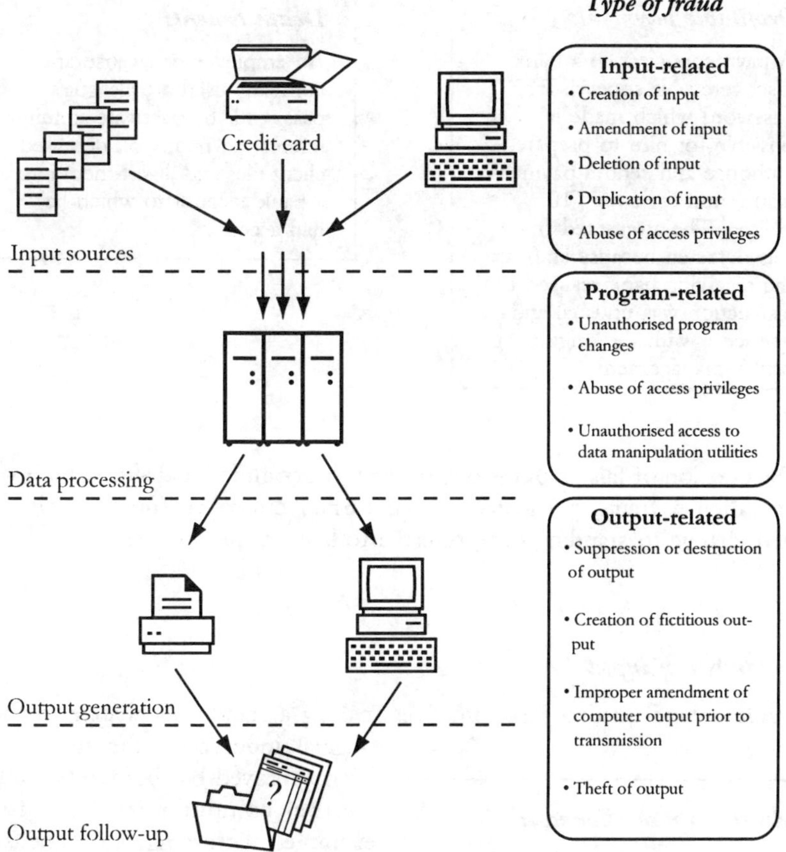

Input related computer fraud requires knowledge of how the information is input into the computer system and the supporting clerical and approval processes (for example, what steps are required to add a new supplier or a new employee to the system and are there any controls to highlight the change?).

A brief description and examples of input-related fraud are given in the following paragraphs.

Creation of input

This involves the creation of input in the correct format and type to be included with existing input (or submitted on its own) without detection. This could be as simple as inserting an additional expense requisition into an existing batch or the direct entry of a sales order into a sales entry system. There may be no paper copy of the input as many modern systems allow direct on-line entry of data.

Profitable payments

A payments clerk in a bank discovered his supervisor's password which made it possible for him to prepare, authorise and send a payment instruction for over £10 million. The attempted fraud was detected because staff at the receiving bank realised the instruction was unusual and queried it with the originating bank's management.

Death benefits

An employee of an insurance company used a colleague's passwords to reactivate annuity interest payments on deceased client files and divert them into a bank account to which he had access.

The creation of false input is one of the most common and simple ways of perpetrating a fraud, particularly when carried out in conjunction with a related change to standing data, referred to later in this chapter.

Amendment of input

Amendment of existing input involves making a fraudulent change to the original input after the item has been approved but before its input to the computer system, for example, increasing an expense claim or changing the name and address of a loan applicant.

Multi-purpose phonecard

Several years ago a bank received complaints from customers about phantom withdrawals from one particular cash machine. The bank installed video cameras which recorded the culprit inserting phonecards after other customers had withdrawn their genuine cards. A fault in the cash machine software meant that cards inserted into the machine immediately after a transaction were assumed to belong to the previous customer and permitted further transactions on their account. The criminal had discovered the fault by accident. The fault affected only a handful of machines which were all shut down until the software was fixed.

Interesting discount

A data entry clerk reduced the interest rate on specific personal loan application forms when entering them into the bank's computer. In return the applicants paid the clerk 50 per cent of the value of the interest saved.

Deletion of input

> **Employees not terminated**
>
> A payroll employee regularly destroyed employee termination notices and then changed the bank account details for the payment of salary. The fraud was not detected until he was taken ill.

The deletion of input prior to its entry or capture into the system could be as simple as the removal as an item from a batch of records or the deletion of the entire batch.

Duplication of input

Duplication of input is a simple but effective way of having selected information (e.g., request for payment or stock shipment) processed more than once with the extra transaction being channelled to the credit of the perpetrator. The process of duplicating input may involve copying input and submitting both the original and the copy or simply re-inputting the original document in a later cycle if there is no cancellation of processed items.

> **False applications for refund**
>
> A university employee responsible for the approval of applications for university tuition funds fraudulently obtained over $4.1 million by creating and submitting false applications for refunds.

Warning signs for input-related frauds include:

> **Too many credits**
>
> A data entry clerk processed valid credit notes twice to a particular customer. A friend of the customer would claim a refund for the excess credit and forward a share of the refund to the clerk.

- lack of segregation of duties and responsibilities over the computer systems;
- apparent problems with processing which continually require fixing by a particular member of staff;
- high levels of customer and supplier queries and complaints;
- extensive use of adjusting and other specialist input types to keep accounts in balance;
- unusual transactions occurring on reconciliation suspense reports;
- sharing of passwords;
- passwords not changed regularly/deleted when people leave; and
- clerical and supervisory staff with excessive levels of access (usually justified as required 'just in case something goes wrong').

Input-related computer frauds are dependent on the computer systems functioning correctly. Any changes to the routine pattern of processing, such as a system failure, may lead to the disclosure of the fraud. These frauds occur when clerical controls are ineffective and allow the fraudulent input or change to enter the system or remain undetected. This usually involves a shortcoming of some kind in the segregation of duties.

An important issue to consider in relation to the alteration of input is the type of records that these changes affect. By altering or adding certain types of input the fraud may be converted from a one-off to a recurring fraud which is difficult to detect and, once set up, requires minimal effort by the fraudster to maintain.

A change or addition to transaction input results in a one-off loss. In contrast the alteration of standing data (e.g., increasing an employee's salary) may only require a single change to the input source, but the resultant effect may give rise to a continuing fraud (e.g., overpayment of salaries every month). Similarly, and usually more significantly in loss terms, a fictitious supplier account (e.g., for services, the absence of which is less easily checked than the non-delivery of goods) will allow fraudulent invoices to be processed and paid regularly for as long as the supplier account remains on file.

It is important to distinguish between the alteration of the different types of input as the risks associated with each may be considerably different, requiring different levels of controls to prevent and detect. The alteration of standing input is typically more difficult to detect as the source of the fraud is a single act rather than the recurring action required to fraudulently alter transaction data alone (e.g., fraudulently increase the hours worked on a weekly timesheet).

The table below provides examples of the alteration, addition, deletion and duplication of both standing and transaction data.

Fraudulent procedure	***Examples involving standing data***	***Examples involving transaction data***
Creation of invalid input data	Creation of a bogus employee	Creation of a fictitious invoice from a supplier
Amendment of existing input data	Changes to a customer's discount percentage	Increasing the discount offered to a customer on a one-off order entry form
Deletion of valid input data	Deletion of a valid notice of death of a registered shareholder to enable diversion of dividends	Deletion of a stop payment instruction on a cheque already written but not banked
Duplication of valid input data	Duplication of new insurance policy details (to inflate new business statistics)	Duplication of an invoice for services (as no check against goods received)

Program or system-related computer fraud

Program or system-related frauds involve the illicit manipulation of computer programs or computer operations. Unlike input or output-related frauds, system-related fraud requires a thorough understanding of the information being processed and a sound knowledge of the computer systems involved. Not surprisingly such frauds only accounted for less than one per cent by value of all cases reported in the 1993 survey.

Examples of program-related computer frauds include:

- tampering with a computer program so that it only generates despatch documentation and does not record any entries in the financial records when goods are delivered to a particular customer;
- changing the computer programs so that sales commission is calculated on the basis of gross sales figures before credit notes have been applied.

Loaded lottery

A large lottery system received entries from agents electronically and calculated the winning dividends for each prize pool. The value of each winning entry was calculated by dividing the winning entries by the amount of the prize pool (e.g., 10 winning entries in a $1,000,000 prize pool would each receive $100,000).

During the completion of a scheduled and authorised change to the programs used to calculate the prize pool, a senior programmer also fraudulently changed the program to add an additional prize payout for each lottery, paid to a dummy customer account which he had created (i.e., 11 prizes of $100,000 were paid out).

Due to the lack of controls over reviewing changes to critical programs and a three month delay in reconciling prize pools payouts the fraud remained undetected for a number of months. At the time of detection in excess of $1 million was missing, as was the senior programmer.

Warning signs for program-related computer frauds include:

- changes to programs are poorly controlled;
- no quantitative controls over file contents; and
- lack of physical security over access to computer facilities.

OUTPUT-RELATED COMPUTER FRAUD

Computer systems produce output in many forms. These range from a screen message to hard copy reports or electronic payment instructions transmitted across international borders.

A fraud involving the misuse of output typically involves suppression, fraudulent creation of misleading output or the theft of output which can be used to create value. Like input-related computer fraud this type of fraud does not require a detailed knowledge of the actual computer systems involved but does require a detailed knowledge of the flow of information and the supporting clerical and approval processes (e.g., who receives the exception reports or which printer generates the pre-signed cheques).

Examples of such misuse include the following:

Type of misuse	*Example*
Suppression or destruction of output	Suppression of specific entries on a report highlighting delinquent loan customers at a bank
Creation of fictitious output	Creation of a report containing fictitious or duplicated insurance policies to support inflated new business claims
Improper amendment of computer output prior to transmission	Amendment of payee details on BACS payment tapes between preparation and transmission (for example, by unauthorised access to computer libraries)
Theft of output	Theft of computer generated cheques

In many cases the warning signs of computer fraud will be similar to those applicable to the actual type of fraud being perpetrated as set out in earlier chapters. However, in an environment where computers are extensively used, there are additional indicators which point to the opportunity for fraud or an environment in which fraud might be sustained:

- sharing of passwords may be common practice (therefore password users are not accountable for their activities);
- staff may have excessive levels of access (usually justified as essential when someone is absent or something goes wrong, but again raising the question of accountability and division of duties);
- apparent problems with processing may continually require fixing by a particular member of staff and therefore are not checkable by others;
- staff may make improper use of computer resources (e.g., by accessing the computer systems out of hours);

- improper use may be made of dial-in lines to the computer without proper investigation; and
- there may be large volumes of items or unusual transactions occur in reconciliation or suspense accounts (a natural location for hiding irregular transactions).

Hacking, viruses and software theft

Whilst hacking, computer viruses and software theft are normally classified as computer abuse, their risk to business warrants mention of these issues in relation to computer fraud.

Hacking

Hacking is the term used to describe unauthorised access to a computer system. This may involve the hacker trying to break into a system by guessing an authorised user's password or access code. This could be through a terminal in the company's premises or externally through the telecommunications network often using a dial-in telephone line.

Computer hackers will normally attempt to identify known, and often unprotected, access facilities in the technical software used (e.g., entry points used by software engineers) or seek to spot weaknesses in the company's internal control systems to create the opportunity to gain access to its systems. This may include sifting through refuse for copies of programs or computer documentation which should have been identified as sensitive and shredded.

In some instances hacking can be linked to fraud. One example in Italy involved a group of people using electronic equipment to 'tap' into telephone cables connecting an Automated Teller Machine to a mainframe and 'capturing' the account and PIN numbers as they were transmitted. This information was then used to create fake Automated Teller Machine cards and withdraw money.

In many publicised cases of hacking, the hackers 'caught in the act' have stated that they did not intend to do any damage to the systems involved but simply viewed hacking as 'a challenge'. Others however have attempted (many successfully) to cause damage to systems through sabotage involving the amendment or deletion of critical files or data.

Viruses

A computer virus may be defined as a self-replicating computer program or code used to infect a computer. The virus or code is usually written and hidden within apparently normal programs. It is spread by its introduction to the organisation on a disk or through a network. When the programs concerned are used the virus is activated and runs. It could be as simple as displaying a rude message on the user's screen or as devastating as deleting or corrupting data or files. Often the virus will be programmed to duplicate itself and can therefore affect many or all the computers linked together on a network. In some instances the virus may be triggered by a specific date (e.g., Friday the Thirteenth Virus). In this case the virus lies dormant until the internal calendar on the computer system reaches the trigger date and the virus is then activated.

Prevention is much preferred to cure. Rules prohibiting the introduction of external disks and programs without appropriate safeguards, combined with the use of anti-virus software and appropriate reporting and help-desk procedures, provide some level of protection.

The emergence of viruses is a relatively new problem. To date the majority of viruses have been restricted to the micro computer environment and have been primarily passive (i.e., not causing any direct damage by deleting or corrupting files). This, however, does little to reduce the potential impact of viruses on the business world which is compounded because many companies are now 'down-sizing' their systems to micro-based environments. According to the National Computing Centre the elimination of a single virus from an organisation is estimated, on average, to cost £50,000.

United States studies estimate that computer viruses are costing approximately £2 billion per year and on average each infection affects approximately 142 computers and results in two days of down time. These costs indicate the vulnerability of business systems to viruses. The need for controls in relation to viruses in some businesses may be as important from the perspective of damage and cost as that of fraud. The media publicity from viruses can be particularly damaging.

Invisible customers

An accountant was convicted under the Forgery and Counterfeiting Act after selling illegal copies of an accounting software package. His crime was discovered when the purchasers sought after-sales support from the official package suppliers.

Software theft

Software theft is a criminal activity. The copying of computer software without authorisation violates the UK Copyright, Designs and Patents Act (1988). Software creates unique problems because it is so easy to duplicate.

However, copyright law makes no distinction between duplicating software for sale or for free distribution; the law protects the exclusive rights of the copyright holder. Unfortunately many people regard illegal copying as morally acceptable behaviour and these attitudes leave many organisations vulnerable to legal action under the 1988 Act.

Civil damages for copying unauthorised software can be substantial. Criminal penalties for the manufacture, possession, importation and distribution of illegal software include significant fines and imprisonment. Software theft in the United Kingdom is costing £400 million per year in lost sales to software producers and distributors. The software industry, represented by the Federation Against Software Theft (FAST), is justifiably seeking to recover these revenues and help organisations to reduce the occurrence of illegal copying.

> ***Everything has a price***
>
> In a major manufacturing company a systems manager stole the company's computer files and attempted to blackmail the company by demanding a ransom in exchange for their return. He was apprehended before he could obtain the ransom.

Almost half the organisations that responded to a 1994 survey on software theft conducted by KPMG for FAST believed that illegal copying had occurred in their organisation. However, most respondents had taken steps to reduce the risk of software theft: 82 per cent perform regular inventories of software and 67 per cent match the results of these inventory checks back to original purchase records.

Conclusion

The development of international shared networks, so-called digital superhighways, has increased the opportunities for technically adept criminals. The most popular network in the world is Internet, with an estimated 20 million users worldwide. Although Internet was born out of a US Department of Defense project in the 1970s, security was not a priority until the late 1980s when a student at Cornell University unleashed a rogue program that brought the network down. Internet, also called the 'Net' or the 'Matrix', is a global community with a diverse population ranging from multinational corporations and world famous universities to 'computer nerds' and 'cyberpunks'.

Like any community, Internet has its seedier side. Computer criminals may go 'Net-surfing' through the network to find anything from information services on computer security threats to bulletin boards containing credit card numbers and tips on breaking into cars.

Early in 1994, tens of thousands of secret Internet passwords were stolen which enabled criminals to break into the owners' files and send fraudulent electronic mail messages. Software theft is another widespread crime on the Net. Organisations linking to Internet and other public networks need to realise that, by connecting to the networks without taking proper precautions, they could be walking into an electronic Wild West.

7 FIGHTING FRAUD

Introduction

Fraud is one of many business risks, and like most risks it can rarely be eliminated. However, it can be mitigated and managed to limit the risk and damage. Successful fraud prevention involves creating an environment which inhibits fraud and taking sharp but appropriate action when fraud is found or suspected. The key is to have a coherent strategy. If one element of the strategy is missing, the whole may be undermined.

The key elements we discuss in this chapter are illustrated in the chart below:

Fighting fraud - a coherent strategy

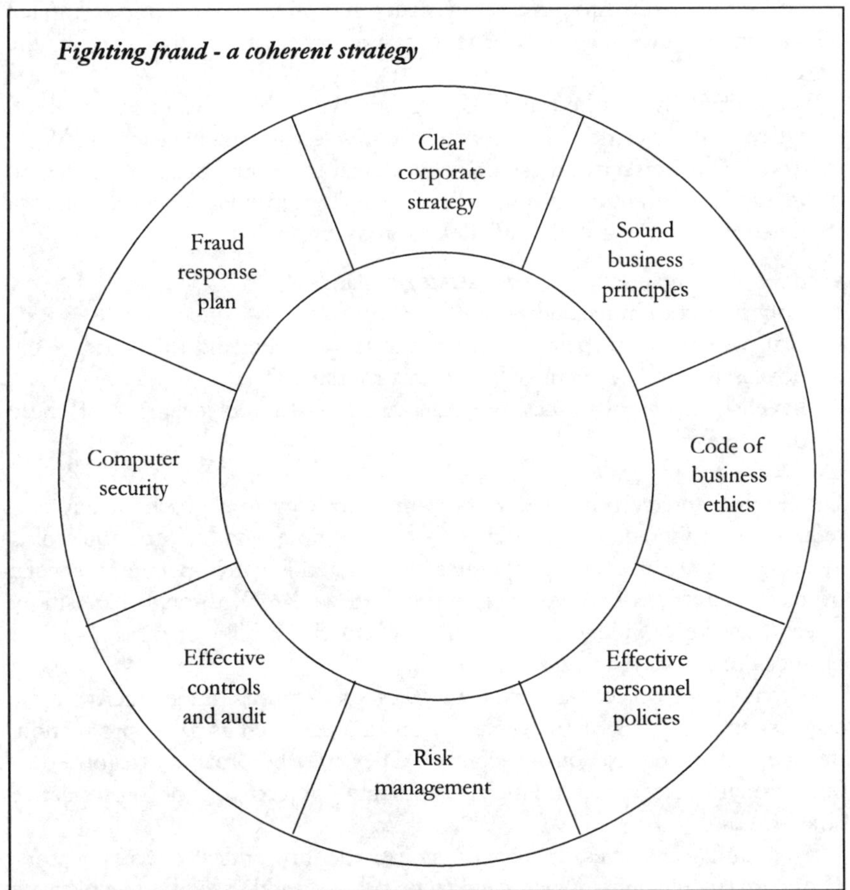

The elements discussed are also applicable to smaller and owner-managed entities. However, certain of the objectives are likely to be implicit in the way the business is conducted rather than being explicitly stated or formally documented. The lack of formal mechanisms should be mitigated by the directors' close involvement in and supervision of the business.

Clear corporate strategy

A clear corporate strategy communicated to all staff is essential not only to the success of the business but also to the fight against fraud. As noted in Chapter 2, poorly defined strategy, while not usually the direct cause of fraud, is often one of the key aspects which defines the environment in which fraud thrives.

Every organisation, whether large or small, has business objectives. These may be set formally through a highly structured process or emerge as implied targets in an informal way. The process depends on the size of the organisation.

The objectives may be classified as group-wide objectives or activity-level objectives. Group-wide objectives include mission statements such as 'We fly to serve'. To be effective these objectives need to be supported by strategies, business plans and budgets otherwise they will not provide practical guidance to lower management and staff. Relevant issues are:

- does the organisation have a strategic plan?
- how is it communicated to staff?
- is it evident from their behaviour that they understand the strategy?
- how is the achievement of objectives measured?
- have sufficient resources been allocated to the achievement of these objectives?

Developing and communicating corporate strategy in a group of any size requires considerable time and effort. The time and effort required is increased where the group operates or is intending to operate in several overseas countries or where the group has grown largely through acquisition. There may be a wide range of cultures and the quality of personnel and business practices may vary considerably.

Activity-level objectives cover the various activities undertaken by the organisation or parts of the organisation in areas such as sales, production, finance, marketing and quality control. They may be broadly categorised as operational objectives, financial reporting objectives and compliance objectives.

By setting objectives, management can identify critical success factors. These are key elements which need to be properly addressed if objectives are

Activity-level objective	***Example***
Operational objectives	• Ensure adequate supply of raw materials • Develop new technology to design products for market needs • Commit resources to projects with highest rate of return
Financial objectives	• Make payments for authorised purchases • Ensure that all services rendered are invoiced in the proper period
Compliance objectives	• Ensure that VAT returns are submitted • Comply with health and safety regulations

to be achieved. If activity-level objectives are not consistent or are not in line with the strategies, business plans and budgets, they will not be supported by all levels of management and staff. They have to be consistent with the group-wide objectives.

Whether the corporate strategy succeeds will depend largely on the ability of the business to manage the risks associated with its strategy. To be effective any fraud prevention strategy needs to be integrated with and reflect the risks inherent in the objectives and strategy of the organisation as a whole. We discuss the ways in which the risk of fraud may be managed below.

Sound business principles

A number of groups have adopted a formal statement of business principles to define the general principles which govern the way the group conducts its affairs. Typically, the principles relate both to corporate decision making and to the behaviour expected of employees in conducting the group's business.

". . . Business ethics are not negotiable – a well-founded reputation for scrupulous dealing is itself a priceless company asset and the most important single factor in our success is total adherence to our beliefs.

"Some employees might have the mistaken idea that we do not care how results are obtained, as long as we get results. This would be wrong: we do care how we get results. We expect compliance with our standards of integrity throughout the company, and we will support an employee who passes up an opportunity or advantage which can only be secured at the sacrifice of principles."

Source: Institute of Business Ethics

A major United Kingdom food group introduces its statement of business principles as shown on page 121.

The content of a typical statement of business principles is set out below.

Statement of business principles – outline

1 **Preface or introduction** (signed by the Chairman or Chief Executive, or both) A sentence on the purpose of the statement – the values which are important to the top management in the conduct of the business such as integrity, efficiency, professionalism and responsibility. The role of the company in the community and a personal endorsement of the statement and the expectation that the standards set out in it will be maintained by all involved in the organisation.

2 **Key areas to include**

- *The objects of the business*
  The service which is being provided – a group of products or a set of services – financial objectives and the business' role in society as the company sees it.
- *Customer relations*
  The importance of customer satisfaction and good faith in all agreements. The priority given to customer needs, fair pricing and after sales service.
- *Shareholders or other providers of money*
  The protection of investment made in the company and proper 'return' on money lent. A commitment to effective communication with this group of people.
- *Suppliers*
  Long term co-operation. Settlement of bills. Joint actions to achieve quality and efficiency.
- *Employees*
  How the business values employees. The company's policies on recruitment, organisation, development and training, communication, work conditions, safety, industrial relations, employment opportunity, retirement, severance and redundancy.
- *Society or the wider community*
  Compliance with laws. The company's obligations to conform to environmental constraints. Involving staff in corporate policy, education and charities. Role of the business. Standards within the organisation and in dealings with others.
- *Other matters*
  Relations with development policy and management. The ethical standards expected of employees (detailed guidance will usually be in a separate code of business ethics).

Source: Institute of Business Ethics

The precise form and content of the statement will depend upon the particular business but preparing the statement is only a first step. To be effective the key messages in the statement need to be integrated into every aspect of the company's culture, through induction and training programmes and its day-to-day operations. Once again where a business is operating in several overseas countries and has grown largely through acquisition it will require considerable effort to instill consistent business principles throughout the group.

Code of business ethics

Fraudsters often justify their frauds as 'taking their dues' or claim what they did was accepted practice or was condoned by management. Closing these 'defences' makes fraud harder. A code of business ethics should be relatively short and written in simple language. Ideally it should be concerned with problems experienced by employees and include something about the procedures to be followed when they are confronted with an ethical dilemma at work. It should make clear what will happen if the code is breached.

The content of a typical code of business ethics is set out on the following page.

A number of companies require employees to sign a copy of the code of business ethics when they join the company and annual statements of compliance. Whether or not companies wish to do this will be a matter of policy. Remember, however, that failure to do so may mean that employees may be or may claim they were unaware of company policy. This may be significant in dismissal or disciplinary proceedings. As with statements of business principles, the code is only a starting point. Integration of the code into the company's day-to-day operations is the key. Management should continually demonstrate, through words and actions, a commitment to high ethical standards and should understand how employees will interpret that message.

A small company may not have a written code of business ethics but that does not necessarily mean that it could not have a culture that emphasises the importance of integrity and ethical behaviour. Through the visible and direct involvement of the owner/manager, the commitment to integrity and ethical behaviour can be communicated orally, in staff meetings and one-to-one discussions.

Code of business ethics – outline

1 Introduction
A statement setting out why the code has been produced and its status, e.g., that it applies to all employees and that any non-compliance will be considered a serious disciplinary matter.

2 Conflicts of interest
This section should include such matters as interests in organisations with which the company does business such as directorships, employment of close family members or a significant shareholdings. There should be a policy that all such potential conflicts should be reported to a nominated independent senior officer and recorded. There should also be a ban on share dealing as a result of information obtained in the course of work for the organisation.

3 Giving and receiving of gifts
There should be specific guidance on the giving or receiving of cash, goods, services, hospitality or bribes in any form. There should also be a company policy on the offering of gifts to others and the level of hospitality that is acceptable to offer or receive. There should also be a direction that any gifts offered or received should be reported to a superior and recorded.

4 Confidentiality
This section should deal with information which is obtained in the course of work and non-disclosure of such information to unauthorised persons, etc.

5 Working environment
This section should deal with standards for the working environment of employees and health and safety considerations, etc.

6 Equal employment opportunity
Selection for a position in the company shall be based on suitability for the job and that there will be no discrimination purely on grounds of race, religion, marital status, sex, colour, nationality, disability or ethnic or national origin. Similar undertakings on promotion and security of employment.

7 Other areas
Other areas which may be covered include political activities by individuals, obligations under competition or anti-trust laws, 'moonlighting' by employees and sexual harassment.

Source: Institute of Business Ethics

The topics included in the statement of business principles may be included within the Code of Business Ethics. A checklist and illustrative code of business ethics is available from The Institute of Business Ethics (see list of further reading).

Effective personnel policies

In the introduction to this guide we noted that more than half of recorded corporate fraud is committed by management and employees, or in collusion with insiders. Personnel policies are a key element in developing the right culture and deterring fraud. The three most important aspects are:

- recruitment screening;
- appraisals; and
- exit procedures.

Recruitment screening

Fraud by management or employees is sometimes a sign of failure in the recruitment process. With hindsight the information supplied by the employee may be found to have been false or misleading. Two examples of bogus curriculum vitae were given in the section on *Other frauds* in Chapter 4.

More thorough checking of information and references provided by applicants may reduce the number of dishonest staff; it will also convey to all new recruits the company's attitude to dishonesty.

Effective recruitment screening includes:

- segregation of the recruitment and the screening process wherever possible;
- independent verification of employee details and references (original documents should be verified as these can easily be faked; copies should never be accepted);
- oral confirmation of references;
- investigation of gaps in employment history;
- involvement of an independent observer at interviews – grandiose claims should be put to the test; and
- probing of evasive replies.

It is surprising how often one or more of these basic procedures is omitted.

Sometimes recruitment screening can be exceptionally weak. In one investigation it was noted that the personnel file of a senior official was almost completely empty, the individual apparently having joined the company some years previously on the strong recommendation of the head of department. It later transpired that the head of department had committed various frauds over a number of years. Possibly there was an ulterior motive for the 'recommendation'.

Recruitment screening should extend to temporary staff and to

> **A temporary accounts assistant**
>
> A gang which was involved in cheque fraud used to plant a temporary accounts assistant at various companies. The temp used to obtain cheques awaiting signature left unattended, cancelled cheques and returned cheques and other documents including authorised signatures. Sometime later two of the gang's forgeries hit the bank account of one of the companies, having passed through the central clearing system.

contractors, who often have the same access to assets and accounting information as permanent employees. They need to be subject to the same level of scrutiny. As a minimum the company should ensure that an agency's screening procedures are comparable to its own. The example opposite illustrates how easily organised criminals may infiltrate a company.

Cleaners, caterers, messengers and service engineers also have access to premises and are rarely challenged. Companies should ensure that employers of such service staff have checked their credentials.

Appraisals

Regular appraisal of employees is not only important to monitor performance and to discuss career development but also to give employees the opportunity to air grievances and discuss other problems. Such interviews may provide the first clue that all is not well in a particular department, for example concerning low morale or the way a department is run.

Exit procedures

We noted above the importance of setting clear, unarguable policies and guidelines on conduct. A well publicised intention to pursue all those found to have defrauded the company and to report the matter to the police is equally important. A history of such action is doubly effective.

Fraudsters should be left in no doubt of the company's willingness to take legal action and of the consequences for their continued employment, their pension and their other assets.

Employees suspected of fraud need to be dealt with according to their contracts of employment. Sometimes there may be difficulties if these do not, for example, provide for immediate suspension on suspicion of fraud, or if the nature of prohibited activities and conflicts of interest is not made clear.

All employees should be interviewed by someone other than the employee's normal line manager when they leave. Sometimes departing employees are a good source of information.

> ***A dishonest manager***
>
> During an investigation staff who had recently resigned were interviewed. Several commented adversely on the character of their immediate manager: one stated that he was unwilling to work for a dishonest manager and provided evidence of specific frauds. Later it became evident that others in his department knew of his dishonesty, at least in part. It therefore gave employees a potentially dangerous message when he was not prosecuted, instead being relieved of his duties with an agreed form of words in his reference.

Risk management

A management team that is alert to the possibility of fraud and which conducts itself accordingly on a day-to-day basis is a powerful deterrent to fraudsters, both within and outside the company. However, many companies do not assess the risk of fraud in a systematic way. The analysis of the risks may be haphazard concentrating only on certain external risks or focusing too much on procedures and controls rather than the specific risks of fraud which the company faces. As a result there may be significant areas of unmanaged risk and the possibility that significant fraud may remain undetected for several years.

Managing the risk of fraud needs to be considered in the context of a company's approach to risk management more generally. If the company's assessment of general business risks is weak or poorly structured any attempt to manage the risk of fraud is unlikely to be successful.

In any business, management needs to understand the major risks that the business faces if they are to avoid significant adverse impacts from unexpected and uncontrolled events. Management need to identify areas of risk, assess the likelihood of an adverse event arising and consider the potential impact of such an occurrence. This provides a basis upon which management can decide to accept the risk and run with it or take steps to minimise it.

Many general business risks have implications when assessing the risk of fraud in the business. Therefore any attempt to analyse and manage that risk needs to be integrated with the company's approach to managing risk more generally.

In the chart on the following page we identify the key aspects which need to be considered when assessing the risk of fraud. The precise way in which these elements are integrated into the wider risk management process will depend on the approach adopted to risk more generally by the particular organisation.

The key to the approach is the order in which it is applied: begin with risk and end with controls – never the other way round.

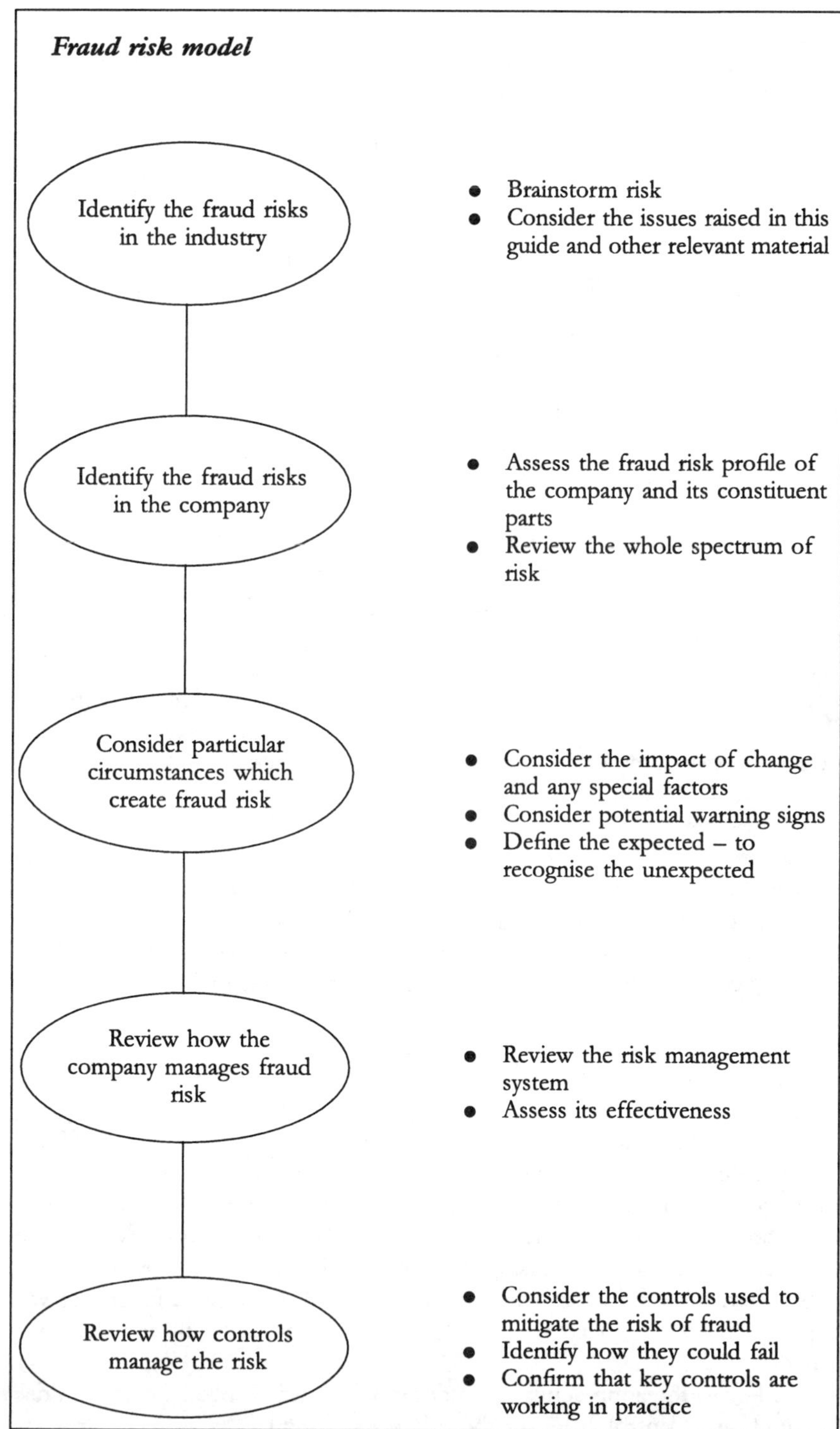
Fraud risk model
Identify the fraud risks in the industry
• Brainstorm risk
• Consider the issues raised in this guide and other relevant material
Identify the fraud risks in the company
• Assess the fraud risk profile of the company and its constituent parts
• Review the whole spectrum of risk
Consider particular circumstances which create fraud risk
• Consider the impact of change and any special factors
• Consider potential warning signs
• Define the expected – to recognise the unexpected
Review how the company manages fraud risk
• Review the risk management system
• Assess its effectiveness
Review how controls manage the risk
• Consider the controls used to mitigate the risk of fraud
• Identify how they could fail
• Confirm that key controls are working in practice

Identify the risks in the industry

The first step is to consider the extent to which external factors such as technological developments, the changing needs of customers, increased competition, new legislation or regulations or economic changes, may also increase the risk of fraud. For example, technological developments may radically change the cost structure or increased competition may squeeze margins and put pressure on liquidity. These factors in turn may provide the motivation for the manipulation of results.

It is then necessary to consider whether certain types of fraud may be particularly prevalent in the particular industry. For example, in a large manufacturing or contracting business, procurement fraud may be a major issue. The way business is conducted may also result in particular risks, for example the extensive use of agents and intermediaries, such as in the insurance or travel industry.

Every industry is affected by specialised types of fraud and these need to be identified. These frauds often relate to the abuse of a particular product, for example, credit cards in banks, telephone systems in the communications industry or ticket fraud in the airline industry.

Brainstorming of industry risk should, where possible, involve senior personnel from a range of disciplines, not just financial staff. Valuable information may also be gained from the relevant industry association or by informal links with other similar companies in the industry.

Identify the fraud risks in the company

The next step is to focus on the particular risks in the company itself. There are two key aspects to consider:

- general factors which may make the company more susceptible to fraud; and
- specific risks of fraud to which the company may be exposed.

In Chapter 2 we identified some of the general factors which may make a company more susceptible to fraud. These factors relate to the personnel, the culture, the structure and the business profile of a company. Assessing these risk factors is sometimes quite difficult. The risk profile needs to be assessed regularly and, once again, senior staff from a range of disciplines need to be involved.

The second step is to consider the specific fraud risks to which the company may be exposed in particular those identified in Chapters 4 and 5 of this guide.

In larger groups this process will need to be replicated across all the main operating divisions and companies. It is important to remember that there may be high risk areas in relatively low risk groups. For example, the risk profile of a particular manufacturing group may be relatively low but the risk profile of its treasury operations may be high, for example, because complex derivative products are being used by relatively inexperienced staff without adequate policies and guidelines or sufficient understanding of the risks involved in their use.

Identify particular circumstances which may increase risk

It is important to consider particular circumstances which may increase risk. As we explained in Chapter 2, the risk profile of a company can change very quickly due to changes in circumstances. Examples of such conditions include:

- changed operating environment;
- new personnel;
- new or revamped information system;
- rapid growth;
- new technology;
- new products or activities;
- corporate restructuring; and
- new foreign operations.

In Chapter 2 we gave some examples of the problems which may occur.

Review how the company manages fraud risk

As noted in the introduction to this chapter, the key to fighting fraud is to have a coherent strategy. If one of the elements is missing then the whole strategy may be undermined. For example, it is quite possible for a company to have a successful business strategy, apparently sound business principles and ethics and a reasonable system of internal controls but still be very exposed to the risk of fraud. The company's assessment of risk may be limited, its recruitment screening may be weak or it may not have an effective fraud response plan and therefore not respond properly to fraud alerts.

It is therefore important that the company looks at all aspects of its fraud prevention strategy not only in relation to its existing business but also in connection with planned expansion or new ventures, for example in new overseas markets. What infrastructure will the business teams going into those new markets take with them? Are the defences of the group consistent across its various businesses or have they been developed in a haphazard way with no common benchmarks?

The occurrence of fraud might be evident from key financial indicators, for example major stock losses or significant bad debts. However, monitoring of other indicators will be necessary to identify high risk situations or areas of potential fraud. For example, management information on the prices and terms given to customers and suppliers, changes to standing data, monitoring dormant accounts, customer complaints, the volume of credit notes and adjustments on accounts and the ownership of supplier companies is important. Many of these features need to be reviewed on a regular basis so that senior management can fully monitor the profile of customers and suppliers. In some cases it may not be clear that a 'loss' has been suffered, for example in many types of procurement fraud, where the 'loss' is the difference between the price which the company has paid and the price which it would have paid if inside information had not been leaked to the favoured supplier by its employees. In these cases it is necessary to look at the prices and terms and the nature of the activity on particular accounts in order to identify whether anything is unusual.

It is crucial to measure how well the risks are being managed and ensure that responsibilities are clearly defined. To be effective these measures need to cover a range of factors, not just measures of profit and loss. A number of groups are implementing a broader range of targets and measures using a 'balanced score card' approach. Certain groups are also introducing benchmarking, minimum standards which must be met across the group, allowing individual companies to define the precise way in which they will manage the risk and meet the minimum standards.

In many large 'entrepreneurial' groups there is a strong sense of identity and 'ownership' in individual operating subsidiaries. Some of these measures may be perceived as undue interference in their activities at group level. They need to be sold on the basis that they provide a helpful framework within which risks may be assessed more effectively and streamlined control objectives set. Any group needs to make clear what it considers an acceptable level of risk. Improved risk management is a way of protecting profit not creating cost.

Review how controls manage the risk

Finally, at a more detailed level businesses need to assess how effective internal controls are in managing the risk of fraud. Internal controls often fail because they are developed in a haphazard fashion without taking account of the whole spectrum of risk. Controls need to be developed in a structured way, based on the key risks identified in each area of the business. It is quite common to find a wide range of standards and practices for similar businesses in large groups.

Of course there is always a cost associated with controls. Companies need to balance the perceived risk against the cost of the control. Unfortunately, the comparison is quite often not accurately performed as it is much easier to estimate the cost of the controls than the nature and extent of the risk. We discuss controls in more detail below.

Effective controls and audit

Many companies have controls which are good in theory but not in practice. This may be because the people who operate the controls shortcut them to save time or because, although faithfully carried out, the control is no longer the right one. No system of controls can prevent every fraud but companies where controls are kept under review and are updated are the least susceptible.

Sometimes the full implications of weaknesses in control are not appreciated. Weaknesses may be looked at in isolation and the level of risk not fully appreciated. For example, a particular company seemed to be quite well controlled. However, a number of weaknesses were identified in the purchases area including:

- no competitive tendering procedures for non raw material purchases;
- poor budgetary control over such purchases;
- weak supplier account opening procedures and no review of amendments made to standing data;
- a very large number of dormant supplier accounts; and
- weak cheque signing procedures – bank mandate not clear, with many cheques over the cheque signing limit being signed by one cheque signatory rather than two.

What was not fully appreciated was that these weaknesses facilitate most of the purchasing frauds discussed in Chapter 4. It is important to consider fully the implications of control weaknesses taken together. It is also important to focus on the specific warning signs of fraud discussed in Chapter 4.

Highlighted on the following page are some of the ways in which internal controls may be undermined based on the guidance given earlier in this guide.

Internal audit time is often taken up with identifying the controls in a given business and performing walk-through tests to confirm, prima facie, that controls exist. However, in a well-controlled group management should be able to demonstrate to internal audit the key risks which are managed, the controls in place in each area and the measures which have been taken to ensure that the controls are operating effectively in practice. If management's responsibilities are well-defined in this area more of internal audit time may be used to focus on high risk areas and perform, when appropriate, work of a

Factors which may undermine controls

	Potential problem	*Comments*
1	Autocratic management style	Management override. Transactions dealt with outside the main system.
2	Unquestioning obedience of staff	Procedures followed by rote or staff acquiesce or collude in fraud.
3	Employee groupings undermine segregation of duties	Employees may have worked together before in countries or companies with poor business morality.
4	Poor quality staff	Internal controls are only as effective as the people operating them.
5	High staff turnover	Inadequately trained, may lack experience, will not have absorbed the culture of the company.
6	Low morale	Unhappy staff are less likely to operate controls effectively.
7	Results at any cost	Corners may be cut and results manipulated to ensure achievement on paper.
8	Manuals and procedures poorly structured	Controls not linked to key risks which face the business in each area.
9	Responsibility not linked to accountability	Manuals need to tie in closely with individual job descriptions. Each member of staff needs a clearly defined package of procedures and controls for which he or she is responsible.
10	Too many procedures and controls	Bureaucracy. Too many procedures, controls, authority limits, etc. This usually happens where a risk-based approach has not been followed. Staff will try to by-pass the system.

specialist nature when there are indicators of fraud or high levels of risk associated with absent controls.

Computer security

Computer fraud can be prevented or discouraged through well designed, properly implemented and maintained internal controls over the information systems. As explained in the previous chapter the larger exposures in relation to computer fraud involve manual processing, so a combination of both manual and computer based controls will usually be required.

Controls need to be thought about in the early stages of developing new systems as it is often difficult and expensive to change the systems once they have been designed or implemented. In fact, as systems are becoming more integrated, the need for an overall security framework, with which all new systems must comply, will increase. Without a framework different systems will have inconsistent levels of control.

The British Standards Institute (BSI) has recently published a code of practice for information security management which has been developed in conjunction with the DTI and a group of leading British companies. This provides a useful framework for implementing and managing information security and includes ten key controls that most organisations should aim to achieve. These are shown opposite:

1 **Information security policy document**

A written policy document must be available to all company employees responsible for information security.

2 **Allocation of information security responsibilities**

Responsibility for the protection of individual assets and for carrying out specific security processes must be explicitly defined.

3 **Information security education and training**

Users should be given adequate security education and technical training.

4 **Reporting of security incidents**

Security incidents must be reported through the correct channels as quickly as possible.

5 **Virus controls**

Virus detection and prevention measures and appropriate user awareness procedures must be implemented.

6 **Business continuity planning process**

There must be a managed process in place for developing and maintaining business continuity plans across the company.

7 **Control of proprietary software copying**

Copyright material must not be copied without the owner's consent.

8 **Safeguarding of company records**

Important company records must be safeguarded from loss, destruction and falsification.

9 **Compliance with data protection legislation**

Applications handling personal data (on individuals) must comply with data protection legislation and principles.

10 **Compliance with security policy**

Systems must be regularly reviewed to ensure compliance with company security policies and standards.

Source: 'A Code of Practice for Information Security Management'

Risk	**Possible preventive controls**
Input-related fraud	• Segregation of duties in user areas and between users and IT staff • Independent reconciliations • Authorisation of changes to standing data • Access controls over data files • Periodic listing and review of standing data
Program-related fraud	• Authorisation and testing of program changes • Restricting access to system libraries containing live programs • Using special utility programs to compare changed versions of programs to original versions to make sure that only authorised amendments have been made • Reducing dependence on key systems staff
Output-related fraud	• Segregation of duties in user areas • Independent reconciliations • Good custodial controls over sensitive stationery • Good access controls
Hacking	• 'Fire walls' – dedicated systems to handle external communications that act as a safety barrier between external networks and the organisation's own computers • Computer screens should not show your organisation's name • Monitoring communications lines for unusual activity
Viruses	• Use up-to-date anti-virus software on personal computers and local area networks • Education and awareness campaigns to ensure that all staff are aware of the risks and their responsibilities • Contingency plans for limiting damage when a virus is discovered
Software theft	• Education and awareness campaigns to ensure that staff are aware of their responsibilities and the penalties for breaking the law • Maintain good records of software purchases and licence agreements • Conduct periodic software audits and reconcile the results against inventories of purchases

Examples of controls that will help to prevent some of the specific risks discussed in Chapter 6 are set out opposite.

Fraud response plan

A fraud response plan is a document setting out the policies and procedures guiding a company's response to major fraud or theft. It may form part of an overall crisis management plan, but in all cases its purpose is to enable prompt and effective action to be taken to:

- minimise the risk of subsequent losses;
- improve the chance and scale of recoveries;
- reduce any adverse commercial effects;
- demonstrate that the company retains control of its affairs in a crisis; and
- make a clear statement to employees and other parties that it is not a soft target for attempted fraud.

An effective fraud response plan should be closely tailored to each company's particular circumstances and business philosophy. It should reflect the nature and scale of likely losses. It should cover both statements of general policy and specific steps to be taken in the event of major fraud, for example:

- corporate policy on fraud and theft by employees and others;
- the person to whom fraud should be first reported;
- procedures for securing assets and accounting (and operational) records;
- legal and personnel procedures;
- contact with police, insurers, regulatory authorities and the press; and
- whom to contact for assistance.

Many companies have no fraud response plan and cannot respond to actual or attempted fraud to their best advantage. Problems which can arise include:

- inadequate communication so that action is late or inappropriate;
- lack of leadership and control so that investigators and advisors are not properly directed and waste time and money;
- failure to react fast enough so that further losses are incurred or the evidence required for successful recovery or prosecution is lost;
- press speculation affecting the share price or supplier or customer difficulties.

The plan must identify those responsible for dealing with major fraud and their authority to do so. Whether fraud is a matter for financial personnel or operational management will depend on the company but must be resolved in advance.

The plan needs to be realistic and commercial. Each company needs to consider both recovery of losses and the issue of crime and punishment in setting its objectives. Each individual case of fraud will need to be considered separately. Recovery of losses and punishment of fraudsters are not always entirely compatible.

Key to any fraud response plan is the identification of an appropriate senior official who will have clear responsibility for dealing with fraud. Employees, suppliers and customers must know who this individual is and how to contact him. Employees need a realistic means of reporting suspicions to a responsible senior officer, without fear that the information will be abused. Some companies have found a confidential telephone line for 'whistle blowers' is useful.

Sending out the right message

A branch of a multinational suffered an equipment procurement fraud. The branch was reluctant to pursue the matter, fearing adverse publicity. However, the main board decided this approach sent the wrong message to other employees. Therefore the employee was pursued, both on a criminal and civil basis, even though the costs of the investigation exceeded the likely recovery. This was judged vital to the interests of the organisation and sent an important message to other employees.

Recovery in full

The assets of a fraudster who had commited a customer fraud on a bank were blocked. As a result the fraudster was persuaded to repay all the money defrauded, together with the costs of the investigation. The overwhelming objective of the bank in this case was the recovery of its losses.

Fraudsters often test a fraud by making several small deniable or inconsequential attempts before a single large transaction. Detection of small frauds may indicate more substantial attempted fraud. It is therefore vital to react quickly and effectively.

Anonymous letters are surprisingly common. They may be malicious and unsubstantiated but they may also reflect disquiet on the part of employees, customers or suppliers. They should always be taken seriously.

For example, it is not uncommon to receive anonymous letters which state that an individual is perpetrating exactly the type of fraud which he is actually committing. Quite often such letters are filed away with little or no action taken.

Some of the key steps to be taken when major fraud is discovered are set out on page 140.

Fraud alerts should always be investigated promptly. There will usually be innocent explanations and no fraud, so enquiries should be discreet and fair.

Truth is stranger than fiction

In a case where cash payments were being made to non-existent suppliers for the benefit of a senior manager, two anonymous letters were found on his personnel file alleging just this type of fraud. The letters were dated ten years earlier and about £100,000 had since been lost.

But fraudsters are adept at giving convincing explanations: the essence of fraud is deception and fraudsters are plausible liars. Any investigation must be thorough and extensive enough to ensure that no disquiet remains.

Companies may mistakenly believe that a fraud is an isolated occurrence, confined to one area. Very often though the individual will have been involved in fraud in other areas for which he is responsible. For example, what may start as an investigation into fraudulent expense claims may develop into an investigation of a more significant equipment procurement fraud. It is therefore essential to investigate fully all areas for which the suspected individual is responsible.

Conclusion

As noted at the beginning of this chapter, the key to fighting fraud is having a coherent strategy. If one or more elements are missing this can seriously undermine the other aspects. Completing the missing elements is perhaps the easier part. Implementing the strategy is more difficult. This involves considerable time and effort, requiring whole-hearted commitment from the top of the organisation.

Action list – investigating fraud

Day 1

- Secure the assets at risk either directly or by notifying (for example) banks and other parties holding assets, by withdrawing signing authorities and by removing suspects from positions of authority.
- Counter the immediate threat by suspension and removal of suspects from the premises (and by changing passwords and similar controls).
- Secure accounting and other records, including those held on computer and take back-ups of all the computer data.
- Secure the contents of suspects offices and computer files. Retain originals or, failing this, copies of all personal documents found in suspects' offices.

Week 1

- Start action to trace and secure assets and accounting records under the control of suspects, their associates and key witnesses, if necessary through legal action.
- Start investigation of the fraud and those involved.
- Assess the business implications (for example, breaches of banking covenants or upset suppliers and customers) and take steps to minimise these.
- Inform insurers and start a claim if losses are covered.

Month 1

- Start asset recovery proceedings.
- Contact the police if necessary and appropriate.
- Start personnel procedures to end the employment of fraudsters.
- Identify and correct flaws in accounting and other systems.
- Inform employees, suppliers, customers, the press, investors, regulators and professional advisors where appropriate.
- Assess the accounting implications, including the size of the loss and the necessary accounting adjustments.

8 Conclusion

Introduction

In this final chapter we reflect briefly on some of the broader issues influencing business, its systems and the fight against fraud.

Empowerment

Fifteen years ago the design of internal control systems and the writing of procedures manuals were profitable sidelines for accountants and consultants. Tome-like binders would contain step-by-step analyses, supported by flow charts, of each of the control systems, often accompanied by narrative notes. Are we still mentally living in the era of procedures manuals when considering the subject of internal controls?

A recent book by leading United States management guru Tom Peters glories under the title *'Liberation management: Necessary Disorganisation for the Nanosecond 90s'*. Peters' prescriptions – the flat organisation, team working, sub-contracting, outsourcing, speed of implementation – are now in increasingly widespread use. Underlying these ideas is the concept of the empowered manager, involving much greater responsibility for devolved subsidiaries or divisions, with high rewards for success but fairly rapid retribution for failure.

This type of structure can lead to much improved results but, from a control perspective, the empowered 'managers' who spring to mind are certain dominant executives who have featured in some recent reported fraud cases. Perhaps these extreme examples are exceptions which do not prove the rule. But this thought is soon put aside by the words of a chief internal auditor of one of the UK's major manufacturing companies who told us recently that creative accounting in subsidiaries is currently one of his group's main risks.

Empowered management teams, not surprisingly, prefer high rewards to dismissal and may not need a great deal of further encouragement to manipulate their results. This would be problem enough, but other members of staff in the business concerned will soon note that their managers are manipulating results to increase their rewards and will themselves, even if they do not indulge in fraud, be less likely to report possible indicators of fraud elsewhere in the organisation.

Downsizing and delayering

Information technology has taken much longer to make a major impact on staffing of organisations than was expected in the early days of computerisation, but it is now leading to change on a massive scale. One of the main effects, from a controls point of view, has been the widespread elimination of middle management in the process known as delayering. The direct effect on controls is that they have all too often walked out of the door with those made redundant, whilst the reorganisation plans which led to change rarely incorporated provision for the replacement of controls which were lost.

More importantly, a new culture of impermanence has been created in many large organisations. Until relatively recently those joining many of the United Kingdom's major companies expected to have a job for life. It is patently obvious that this is no longer the case. Whilst those that remain are no doubt pleased to have kept their jobs, they may well remain in fear of losing them, and question whether the organisation which they expected to remain loyal to them through a long career really deserves their own loyalty in return. These psychological conditions are not ones which encourage 'whistle blowing'.

Of course downsizing and delayering have not taken place merely out of management fashion or as a result of technological opportunities. Much of it has been driven by the need to reduce costs. Such an environment is unlikely to be responsive to demands from controllers or auditors for new controls which are bound, at least on the face of it, to cost money. Those responsible for control are forced to look for the minimum level of control, possibly determined by those procedures which demand the least resources, rather than those that are needed most.

Much of the downsizing has been facilitated by the trend towards outsourcing and subcontracting. This has both positive and negative features in terms of fraud risk. Experience is already showing, particularly in the public sector, that outsourcing is creating opportunities for procurement fraud. In industry and commerce, the risks are increased by the demand of the empowered manager who prefers to get the job done, rather than wait for bureaucratic tendering procedures to be completed. On the positive side, it is much easier to define objective standards to control a subcontractor than an employee and, although information may be at risk, much financial fraud risk may in effect be absorbed by the subcontractor.

Internal auditors are not exempt from the pressures created by these influences. They must justify their cost of operating and are likely to find it difficult to perform their dual roles of looking for efficiencies and effectiveness, and at the same time carrying out a level of scrutiny which will deter and detect fraud. With downsizing extending to head offices, resulting in some of the largest organisations running their international affairs from head offices with very limited staff, the trend is towards pushing internal audit down into operating divisions. But to whom will these internal auditors feel their loyalty is due?

Accelerating change

The third theme is that of accelerating change. New risks of fraud and the speed of the criminal in catching up with security devices are both illustrated by the experience of mobile phone operators. Within only a few weeks of the introduction of smart card security devices for mobile telephones, they were widely available in the East End of London, having been imported from the Far East.

Perhaps such a problem is rather exotic for most businesses, but mundane technological change has made massive changes to control systems, which may not have been recognised. In the last decade EDI, electronic banking, fax and e:Mail have all come into widespread use. But who has been updating the procedures manual to take account of their effect on business processes? We suspect (and hope since it is a waste of time) no-one. The key point is that business is changing far too rapidly for the controls of yesterday to be regarded as effective for the problems of today.

Alongside these detailed changes are the major themes of global business. In some industries, such as the food industry, manufacturing is being concentrated to create production units on a European or world scale. This means that other factories are being closed down and disposed of. Management, having taken the decision to close, will often wash its hands of the disposal process, leading to widespread opportunities for fraud at all levels of the entity which is to be eliminated. The opening of East European markets will create many opportunities, but at the same time lead companies into countries in which they have no previous experience, many of which are thought to be highly corrupt, and where they may be dissuaded by local culture from imposing their normal framework of controls.

A new concept of controls?

We have supposedly moved into the soft 1990s, but the culture created by the 'every man for himself' 80s is unlikely to be eliminated so quickly, particularly when the recession may well have reinforced that attitude. As we have sought to illustrate, traditional procedures and controls, even in the unlikely event they are the same on paper, are most unlikely to have remained unchanged in practice. Companies can no longer rely on these traditional forms of controls to provide comfort that their organisations are properly protected from risk of fraud.

Conclusion

In our view the response to this situation cannot be one of increasing internal or external audit scrutiny, nor completing internal control checklists, useful though they may be. The need is to flow with the tide of empowerment and self interest, and put management itself in the front line in the battle against fraud. It is important for directors to appeal to management's self interest by stressing that fraud in the organisation for which they are responsible is likely to be severely career limiting, and that, uncontrolled, fraud can hit their bottom line, and hence their bonus, very hard indeed. They can be equipped for the battle by sensitising them to the risks which their organisation may run, and by using their knowledge of the business to identify the risks in detail and install appropriate measures to fight fraud. This is one of the main challenges for companies in the 1990s, a key aspect of corporate governance.

Digest of cases

SALES

Management and employee frauds

1 Diversion of sales
2 Bogus goods and services
3 Fictitious sales
4 Kickbacks to/from customers
5 Underbilling/underringing
6 Pre-invoicing
7 Teeming and lading/stealing receipts
8 Writing off receivables for a fee

External frauds

9 Long firm fraud
10 Misrepresentation of credit status/use of false names and addresses

Type of fraud	*Examples*	*Warning signs*
Management and employee frauds		
1 Diversion of sales	*Disgruntled director diverts sales* An ex-director of a company, which had been acquired and then divisionalised, who remained with the group after acquisition, set up a rival company. He diverted sales orders to the rival company by making his employer's tenders for contracts uncompetitive and giving poor performance on other contracts, then recommending the rival company to perform the contracts. Management of the parent company realised something was wrong when several staff left the division and the division was underperforming against budget. *Taking a cut* A company exported goods to a particular country through an intermediary. In fact the intermediary company was owned by the sales director's wife. The firm overcharged for import dues and taxes, passing over the correct amounts to the authorities and retaining the rest.	• Recent acquisitions or reorganisations resulting in low morale, conflicts of cultures, demotion of individuals, etc. • Unexplained loss of customers/ high level of customer complaints. • Business patterns inconsistent – e.g., sales reduced, but spares sales constant. • Unexplained stock losses. • No independent review of pricing structures or charges by intermediaries. • Ownership of intermediary companies not checked.
2 Bogus goods and services	*A ferry service without a ferry* A company attempted to run a ferry service. A feasibility plan was prepared, a manager, an accountant and a sales	• Product 'too good to be true' – for example low risk, high return products.

manager recruited and a shipbroker asked to find a suitable ferry for charter. Approximately £100,000 was allegedly taken from customers who were led to believe that the ferry service would operate. In fact the ferry service allegedly had no financial backing, no crew, no port and no ship. It was alleged that the customers' deposits were used to defray the operating expenses of the company.

The holiday homes that never got off the ground

A company allegedly sold thousands of pounds worth of timeshares on properties abroad which were never built. The company advertised the properties in a glossy brochure, featuring well-known sports stars.

It was alleged that the pictures of the supposed complex were of another development and no building work was ever undertaken. The scheme would not have been granted planning permission by the local authorities concerned.

Two unscrupulous estate agents

Two estate agents cheated elderly vendors out of more than £100,000 by under valuing their properties. The owners were persuaded to sell their properties after being told that their houses were subsiding. Subsequently, they were informed that the purchasers (who were bogus) had pulled out. The estate agents then bought the properties and sold them on at twice the prices paid.

- Glossy advertising, etc not supported by independent evidence corroborating the product/service.
- Service or product supplied at a remote location or at a date far in the future.
- Explanation of transaction is complex, with exotic reasons for advantageous pricing.
- Abnormal levels of growth, profitability.
- Customer base vulnerable, easily exploited.
- Up-front payment or deposit required, well in advance of product being supplied.
- One-off ventures. Companies and staff with no track record.

Type of fraud	*Examples*	*Warning signs*
Management and employee frauds	*Further examples ...* Frauds involving bogus products/services occur in many industries. For further examples see *Investment Business* and *Insurance.*	
3 Fictitious sales	*'Manufacturing' sales* A manufacturer of electronic equipment suffered a serious shortfall in sales. One of its distributors agreed to accept invoices for large deliveries. After the manufacturer's year end, and completion of the audit, the manufacturer issued credit notes to the distributor and took back the stock. *Dummy invoices* A company issued dummy invoices for stock which was old, on sale or return or display and the profit recognised although no payment was expected. Old invoices were redated so that the aged debt report would show them as current. Dummy cash receipts were posted to the sales ledger to clear outstanding debts and then reversed by new dummy invoices to enable the bank reconciliation to work. *Boosting an earnout* A company had acquired a business on terms whereby the controlling shareholder was retained as managing director	• Depressed market conditions/ excessive pressure to meet targets. • Unusual fluctuations in sales. • High sales in the final quarter. • Unusual number or value of credit notes around period ends. • Large number of journals and adjustments in sales ledger and/ or bank reconciliations. • Circularisation of particular customers refused/customer not replied to circularisation or balance not paid. • Customer not generally known in accounts department/file for customer not in main filing/

and an earnout would be payable to him for the two years following the acquisition. The managing director manipulated profits by paying certain expenses personally and by overcharging customers.

account handled directly by senior manager of staff.

- Evasive answers re movements on particular accounts.
- Changes in activity levels inconsistent, e.g., high sales in period but no change in distribution costs.
- Change in business pattern, such as entry into new, remote market.

4 Kickbacks to/from customers

Splitting the difference

A sales director agreed a reduced price for a particular customer. In fact the undisclosed terms of the arrangement were that the customer would receive half the agreed reduction with the other half being paid personally to the sales director. The prices and other terms for particular customers and products were not independently reviewed.

- No independent review of prices and terms (or changes thereto) for particular customers.
- Customers dealt with outside the main system (e.g., no price information on standing data, file held outside main filing, etc).
- Certain customers dealt with by only one member of staff.
- Alterations on invoices or other documentation.

Type of fraud	*Examples*	*Warning signs*
Management and employee frauds		
5 Underbilling/underringing	Underbilling may involve suppression of invoices, understating quantities despatched or manipulating prices or discounts, usually in return for some kind of kickback to the employee concerned. Underringing of tills is a common problem in the retail sector.	• No sequential control over invoices. • No independent checks on prices. • Weak controls over changes to standing data. No standing data for customer. • Alterations on delivery notes or invoices. • Poor control over 'miscellaneous' sales or receipts - e.g., fixed asset sales, sales of valuable waste, cash sales, inter-branch transfers, rebates, deposits etc. • Any evidence of 'secondary systems' for invoicing. • Poor controls over till rolls. • Certain customers dealt with by only one member of staff.

6 Pre-invoicing

Papering over the cracks

The general manager of a company pre-invoiced sales to hide very poor trading results. He also made insufficient provision for slow-moving stock, representing that orders were in hand for the particular stock lines.

Early completion

A construction company did not take the full profit on contract work until a completion certificate was obtained. Owing to poor results on other contracts, management wished to report a large overseas contract as completed and to take profits, although no completion certificate had been issued before the end of its financial year and certain contractual obligations had not been performed. The contract client was provided with a side letter confirming certain undertakings to the customer in consideration for the issue of the completion certificate.

- Changes in pattern of business.
- Inconsistencies in trading pattern, for example delivery costs do not fluctuate rateably with deliveries.

7 Teeming and lading/ stealing receipts

A 'computer error'

A sales ledger clerk, who also had access to cheque receipts, stole a number of cheques. In due course the invoices became overdue. The individual also dealt with customer complaints. He told the customers concerned to ignore the items on their statements telling them that there had been a 'computer error'. Eventually he had to make a significant transfer from another account to rectify the problem, at which point the fraud was discovered.

- Poor segregation of duties.
- Part-paid items on the sales ledger.
- Numerous journals or other adjustments on the sales ledger or bank reconciliations.
- No independent check of the aged debtors analysis, sales ledger or bank reconciliations.

Type of fraud	***Examples***	***Warning signs***
Management and employee frauds	*A 'creative' accountant* A temporary accountant, who was responsible for credit control, stole cheques payable to his employer. He opened two bank accounts in the name of the company. He paid them into the new accounts. The fraud was concealed for a time by bogus journal entries and teeming and lading of the sales ledger accounts.	• Customer complaints not monitored independently. • No independent review of customers who do not pay or who delay payment. • Unusual uncleared lodgements or other items on bank reconciliations at period ends.
	Delivery men line their pockets Delivery van drivers of a company collected cash and cheques from customers and were responsible for banking the receipts. One driver misappropriated both cash and cheques, submitting only the necessary paying in slips. The fraud was not detected for several weeks because bank reconciliations were not performed regularly.	• Alterations to invoices or frequent issue of 'duplicates' on particular accounts. • Differences between original and duplicate paying-in slips or incomplete details on paying-in slips. Alterations, inconsistent with ledger postings.
	Variations on a theme A company accountant wrote to his bankers asking for a particular account to be closed. The letter was apparently from the directors of the company. However, the signature had been forged. He asked for the balance to be transferred to a new account at a building society account which he had opened. When the sales ledger clerk was away, or unable to collect the cheques, the accountant collected the cheques and banked them in the new account. Some of the diverted	• Differences between paying-in slips, cash book details and ledger postings - number of items, dates, payee details etc.

cheques were concealed by fictitious credit note entries in the sales ledger. For other accounts the data was corrupted and the turnover activity and balance deleted.

Another classic case

A credit control manager had staff under his supervision who passed cash and other entries to the sales ledger. The manager was responsible for producing the aged debtor analysis. On occasion, when his staff were away or otherwise engaged, he stole cash and other receipts and deposited them in his personal bank account. He updated the relevant accounts himself and manipulated the aged debtor analysis.

We prefer cash . . .

A manager of a small branch office agreed with a particular customer that they should settle their account in cash. In return they would be able to buy goods at a reduced price. The manager stole some of the cash and falsified the stock records.

8 Writing off receivables for a fee

For a small fee . . .

A credit control manager agreed with a customer that an outstanding balance would be written off in the company's books and the debt not pursued, providing a fee was paid to him personally. The company had weak procedures regarding the write off of bad debts and the control of recovery proceedings.

- Heavy concentration of provisions/write-offs attributable to one employee or division.
- Bad debt write offs and recovery proceedings not monitored closely by senior management.

Type of fraud	***Examples***	***Warning signs***
External frauds **9 Long firm fraud**	*Here today, gone tomorrow* A fraudster established a small electrical retail business. Initially the business was given limited credit terms by its suppliers. The fraudster paid the bills promptly. In due course he submitted much larger orders and longer credit terms were granted by the suppliers. After about four months, when the fraudster had obtained the maximum amount of credit which he thought he could obtain, he disposed of his stock for cash at knock down prices as rapidly as possible and disappeared with the proceeds, leaving the supplier bills unpaid. *. . . a more complex example* A group of fraudsters, using false identities, set up a number of retail businesses, using off-the-shelf companies. Distinctive headed paper was prepared, orders were placed and credit granted. Some of the credit references given to suppliers were from other companies owned by the fraudsters, who gave glowing references of credit worthiness and financial stability. Again the initial small orders were all paid promptly. Larger orders were then placed and increased credit given. A central warehouse, owned by the fraudsters, but apparently having no connection with them, was used to	• Customer not previously known. • Customer at remote location making face-to-face contact with the supplier unlikely. • Air of unreality about the people running the business, their premises, etc. • Rapidly increasing number and/or size of orders. • No independent checks on who references are.

	collect the goods obtained. The items were then sold to cut price stores and market traders at discount prices. Once again, after a few months of operation, the fraudsters disappeared without trace, leaving the supplier bills unpaid.	
10 Misrepresentation of credit status/use of false names and addresses	As noted in Chapter 4, this type of fraud includes a wide range of practices which involve impersonation or the submission of false or misleading information.	• Poor quality documentation; word processor produced invoices, handwritten documentation, etc. • Use of 'accommodation' offices by new customers.

PURCHASES

Management and employee frauds

1 Bid fixing
2 Kickbacks and inducements
3 Work done/goods supplied for private purposes
4 Dummy suppliers and connected companies
5 Bogus intermediaries
6 Misuse of credit notes, rebates and volume discounts

External frauds

7 Bid rigging
8 Advance fee fraud
9 Short deliveries/goods not supplied
10 Substandard products
11 Billing for work not performed/overbilling

Type of fraud	*Examples*	*Warning signs*
Management and employee frauds		
1 Bid fixing	*Information brokers* Employees in a major civil engineering company passed inside information to 'information brokers' who in turn passed it to one of the bidders for a large contract. The information related to the selection criteria being used by the purchasing company and the prices of other bids. The information enabled the supplier to pitch its bid 10 per cent (representing £20 million) above the price it would otherwise have submitted. *The man who liked to move office* A senior manager at a company, in charge of certain large capital purchases relating to an office move, accepted kickbacks from a particular supplier to favour the supplier's bid. The supplier provided details of these arrangements when they were asked why they could not come up with a better price. *There's only one in it* A manager at a company responsible for choosing a new computer system excluded certain major vendors from the bid process. All but one of the companies invited to tender were technically disqualified for various reasons. In fact the	• Abnormal prices/terms. (specifications which can only be met by one supplier). • Bid prices very close together. • Certain well-known suppliers not asked to tender. No competitive bidding for major purchases. • Pre-qualified suppliers. • Small supplier/large contract. Supplier small relative to size of purchasing company. • Location of supplier unusual: remote supplier used for routine services. • Supplier providing services outside normal range of business. • Tenders accepted after closing date. • High levels of extras/claims by particular suppliers.

manager had received a large kickback from the chosen supplier.

- Changes to prices or terms soon after the contract is awarded. Unsupported charges.
- Large number of invoices for particular supplier just beneath an approval threshold.
- Common names, addresses, solicitors etc between bids.
- Use of brokers/consultants in bid process.
- Normal terms of business waived.
- Procurement staff defensive when questioned about the bid process.

2 Kickbacks and inducements

A 'long-standing' supplier

A supplier paid kickbacks to a buyer to retain the company's business. In fact the supplier did not offer particularly good service and their prices were higher than other suppliers. Moreover, variances from estimates including extra quantities, price changes and other extra charges were not questioned by the buyer's manager.

- Warning signs are as for *Bid fixing* above.

A luxury car and £20,000 in cash

A director of a company allegedly accepted a luxury car

Type of fraud	*Examples*	*Warning signs*
Management and employee frauds	and a payment of £20,000 to favour a particular building company which had tendered for refurbishment work at its offices.	
3 Work done/goods supplied for private purposes	*Keeping the house up to scratch* A maintenance department regularly undertook work at remote locations. They incorporated into their schedule work on their own houses. They removed the necessary materials and supplies from inventory and falsified their time records (even charging overtime for the private work). *When the cat's away . . .* The managing director and finance director of a remote subsidiary company submitted claims for false travel and entertainment and purchased various items for private use. The subsidiary was not closely supervised by the parent company, the main control being cursory review of budgets and limited senior management contact.	• Remote subsidiaries, branches and locations not monitored closely. • Unusual delivery times/methods. • Ambiguous or abbreviated descriptions on invoices. • Overordered or surplus stock lines. • Weak link between invoices and origination of order. • Poor segregation of duties.
4 Dummy suppliers and connected companies	*A phantom transport company* A road haulage manager set up a bogus transport company and over an eight-month period invoiced his employer for £150,000. The manager was authorised to pay firms working for the company without having his decisions	• Few details available of the service provided. • Supplier handled directly by senior member of staff. Supplier not generally known to staff.

queried. He used the cash to buy luxury cars, including a Rolls Royce, foreign holidays and luxurious fittings for his home. He had so many vehicles that he was able to set up a car hire business.

Joint venture problems

A remote joint venture operation was run by a service company which specialised in running the particular type of operation. The director of the company arranged for companies owned by him and his associates to supply goods to the joint venture operation at inflated prices. In fact goods or services were not supplied at all or goods of inferior quality were supplied.

Bogus consultancy and design services

The finance director of an information systems company defrauded the company of £1.5 million over a four-year period. For instance he paid £275,000 for computer consultancy never received. He also paid £348,000 to an interior design company in Florida, falsely claiming that the company had provided services to his employer. In fact the sums were channelled back to him and were used to buy three properties in Florida. He also bought computer hardware and then resold it privately or sometimes gave it away.

An attractice accomplice

The finance director of an electronics firm stole £206,000

- Supplier dealt with outside the normal system.
- Address of supplier is PO box, an accommodation address, a private residence or the same as another supplier.
- Addresses and/or telephone numbers of suppliers the same as addresses or telephone numbers of employees or employees' next of kin.
- Names, addresses or other details the same as employees' previous employer.
- Payee name on cheque is abbreviated.
- Invoices are photocopies, crumpled or completely unfolded, have missing header details (e.g., telephone number, incomplete or no VAT number etc), very abbreviated product or service descriptions, different type faces, alterations or annotations.
- Unfolded invoices.

Type of fraud	**Examples**	**Warning signs**
Management and employee frauds	from his employer. He set up bogus accounts and made payments into them. The payments were made on his behalf by a female member of the accounts department who had been recruited eight months previously as a junior assistant. She had become the finance director's mistress and had been promoted rapidly. The finance director used the funds to buy a holiday home, a new car for his mistress and to clear £40,000 of credit card debts. The fraud was discovered by his deputy who noticed payments were still being made to suppliers whom he knew the company had ceased using. *Dangling debits* The managing director of a small company had sole signing power for the company's bank account. He made payments on behalf of other companies in which he had a significant interest, describing them as deposits in respect of contracts which were to be performed on behalf of the company in due course. He accounted for them as debit balances in the purchase ledger to make them less obvious to his fellow directors. *Teeming and lading with suppliers* The chief accountant of a company obtained the two signatures required to give instructions to a bank to make	• Invoices from various suppliers on similar stationery. • Large number of invoices for particular supplier just beneath an approval threshold. • Numerous contras or other adjustments on purchase ledger. • Numerous entries in suspense accounts during the year. • Confirmation of supplier accounts resisted or unusual conditions suggested. • Supplier does not offer usual discounts and special deals. • Weak account opening procedures. • Poor control over dormant accounts. • Poor control over paid invoices. • No zero-based budgeting.

payments by telex to a supplier. He then altered the payee shown on the instructions to the name of a company which he had formed with a similar name to the actual supplier. Since he was also responsible for dealing with suppliers' accounts he was able to 'teem and lade' payments to the supplier whose payments he had diverted.

- No clearly defined budget holder for the account.

Anonymous letters

A senior official at a company made payments to non-existent suppliers. On reviewing his personnel file two anonymous letters alleging just this type of fraud were found. The letters were dated 10 years earlier. About £100,000 had since been lost. The manager had perpetrated an identical fraud at his previous employer.

5 Bogus intermediaries

These frauds involve the manipulation of prices or quantities or substitution of products by intermediaries.

- Ownership/status of intermediaries not known.
- Reason for intermediary arrangements not clear.
- Vendor complaints not monitored independently.

Type of fraud	***Examples***	***Warning signs***
Management and employee frauds		
6 Misuse of credit notes, rebates and volume discounts	*Pressure to maintain profits* The directors of a company which had recently been acquired, and on whom there was pressure to maintain profits, committed various frauds in collusion with suppliers. The directors arranged for a supplier to issue three credit notes amounting to £150,000 each to be offset against the cost of future purchases from that supplier. Details of the transaction were sent out on a telex belonging to a friend of one of the directors. *A rebate disguised as a 'loan repayment'* A supplier sent a cheque for a volume rebate to the managing director of a company. He paid it into one of the company's dormant bank accounts personally and issued instructions to the bank to transfer the funds to the company's normal trading account. He told the company's accountant that this was some of his own money which he had paid in and that it should be credited to his personal account. The amount was subsequently withdrawn by the director. It appeared that the director had loaned the company some money and that the company had subsequently repaid it.	• Abnormal number or value of credit notes, in particular around the period end. • Volume discounts/rebates due not monitored. • Over ordering/stock surpluses (to trigger volume discounts).

7 Bid rigging

Bid rigging is the manipulation of the competitive bidding process: bidders conspire among themselves to set the prices and terms for particular contracts.

- See *Bid fixing* above.

8 Advance fee fraud

Cheap Ferraris

A car dealer took £3.5 million in deposits from 1100 motorists promising that he would obtain Rolls Royces, Ferraris, Aston Martins and Porches at very low prices. Agents received the deposits from motorists, and after deducting commission, sent the rest of the money to the car dealer. He rarely delivered the cars.

Lost: one oil tanker

A Nigerian lawyer attempted to sell £14 million of crude oil he did not own. He used fake documents to sell a non-existent consignment of almost 1.2 million barrels of Nigerian crude oil to an oil company through the spot market in Rotterdam. He obtained $150,000 from a senior official of the company, allegedly for charter fees, and allowed him to speak to a 'tanker captain' on the telephone, confirming that the consignment was en route to Amsterdam. However, the official became suspicious and tipped off police.

- Abnormally low prices. Offer is 'too good to be true'.
- Non-returnable up-front payment or deposit required.
- All dealings through agents or middlemen. Meetings required in unusual places.
- No independent checks possible on the authenticity of the documentation before the release of funds.
- Complex explanations given for advantageous terms or reasons for undisclosed principal entering into deal.
- Deal involves complex and unusual financial instruments.
- Purported principal is overseas and identity cannot be revealed.
- Agent seeks to conclude the deal unusually quickly.

Type of fraud	*Examples*	*Warning signs*
External frauds		• Often involve foreign agents, banks, governments or some mysterious wealthy person.
9 Short deliveries/goods not supplied	*The guvnor's lost the paperwork* Certain payments were made to the head of a supplying company rather than to the company itself. There was no record of any order for the goods invoiced, the serial numbers of the goods received notes had been altered, most of the alleged deliveries were on a Saturday and none of the deliveries had been recorded in the company's goods received records. Further the supplying company did not have any record of the transactions. *Garbage in garbage out* An employee set up a false supplier and then introduced false GRN's and invoices to generate payments through an automated payment system. Controls over the authorisation of new supplier accounts was very weak and insufficient attention was given to the supporting documentation at the time of approval. *Taking a slice* A catering company operated a canteen at a client's	• Weak goods received procedures and/or security. • Weak account opening procedures. • Weak link between origination of order, receipt of goods and approval of invoice. • No analysis of stock shortages by supplier invoice (reason for shortage may be short delivery). • Deliveries at unusual times or direct to customer. • No regular checks on measuring equipment for evidence of tampering.

premises under contract, the basis of which was that all costs were recharged to the client together with a management fee. The canteen manager colluded with the van driver of a food supplier to invoice larger quantities then had actually been delivered. The surplus was sold and the proceeds split between the canteen manager and the driver.

10 Substandard products

Bought in Hong Kong

An electronics engineer, who was contracted by an approved supplier of a major organisation to supply to that company military-grade adjustable voltage regulators for use in submarine torpedoes, instead sold the company cheap commercial substitutes. The company which was normally sub-contracted to do this work had stopped producing them and therefore an alternative source of supply was required.

The electronics engineer claimed that the components met the relevant military standard. He produced false certificates supposedly issued by the company which normally supplied them and by the United States defence department. In fact the certificates were printed by the engineer. The engineer had told the approved supplier that he had managed to obtain war stock parts from the United States and from the grounded space shuttle programme (in fact they had been obtained from a shop in Hong Kong).

- No rigorous quality checks.
- No independent verification of the credentials or status of the particular supplier.
- Change of supplier at very short notice/rushed jobs, preventing the usual quality checks.
- Size of order/delivery schedule too big/too tight for the supplier concerned.
- Terms require substantial payment in advance of delivery.

Type of fraud	*Examples*	*Warning signs*
11 Billing for work not performed/overbilling	*Little and often* A company had a contract to service a road fleet of vehicles. Under the terms of the contract they were not allowed to make a profit on parts supplied. To make up the 'lost' profit the company allegedly overcharged for parts and labour and also invoiced for work not done. Although the overcharging on individual invoices was small, the company submitted a very large number of invoices under the contract with the result that the total loss suffered was very considerable. *Wrong address* The regional management of a property development company colluded with sub-contractors so that work was invoiced to the company for work performed at sites not belonging to the company. Show house furniture and appliances were also delivered elsewhere or subsequently disappeared from the show homes.	• No pricing checks on invoices. • No checks on whether appropriate volume discounts received. • Vague terms in contracts. • No competitive tendering. • No independent review of the need for goods supplied. • No zero-based budgeting. • No independent review of travel, advertising, consultancy, recruitment, maintenance, hire and leasing charges, by supplier, to assess reasonableness of charge against service provided.

INVENTORY

Management and employee frauds

1 Theft of inventory
2 Theft of returned stock
3 Theft of valuable scrap
4 Metering and weighbridge frauds
5 Manipulation of inventory records (*concealment device*)

Type of fraud	***Examples***	***Warning signs***
Management and employee frauds		
1 Theft of inventory	*Employees putting on weight* Employees at a major car manufacturer stole £2 million of spare parts over a three-year period by taping components to their bodies and taking them out of the factory. A union agreement banned body searches. The stolen parts were collected from the homes of the thieves and taken to a central depot, then sent to a parts dealer nearby. He then sold them to other outlets. The parts were sold in bogus manufacturer's packaging. The fraud was picked up when one of the company's security guards noticed accessories, specifically designed for the production line, on sale in a car showroom. *Competition too close to home* Over a period of eight years four employees of an electrical goods manufacturer stole spare parts from the factory. At first small numbers of parts were stolen. However, by the time the men were caught a lorry, which should have contained scrap plastic, was discovered leaving the factory with £25,000 of spare parts on board. The fraud was masterminded by an electrical salesman, assisted by a lorry driver and forklift driver. The salesman's uncle delivered the stolen parts to shops around the country. The spare parts were sold at discount prices. The	• Unexplained differences between book and physical stock. Stock losses not followed up promptly. • Stock turnover in particular locations inconsistent with the general level of turnover. • Poor margins. • Quantity and quality of goods not checked before delivery driver allowed to leave – especially late, early, at lunchtimes, on Fridays, etc. • Poor segregation of duties between buying, warehousing, goods inward and accounting. • Poor control over stock movements at time of stocktakes – between various branches, goods on consignment or on sale or return.

	racket in stolen parts became so bad that the company found it could not compete with the low prices some dealers were charging for them. *Fell off the back of a lorry* A number of storekeepers and delivery drivers were in collusion at a large retailer of electrical appliances. Electrical appliances were stolen during delivery of appliances from the central warehouse. Surplus appliances were obtained by failing to report appliances delivered in excess of delivery requirements and fake claims were made to the central warehouse that an appliance listed on the delivery documents was not received.	• Delivery drivers regularly go out with part-loaded vehicles. • Delivery drivers regularly do same routes or know their routes well in advance. • Delivery drivers ask for routes to be amended on a regular basis. • No independent follow up of customer complaints – re sub-standard products, delays in delivery, short deliveries, etc.
2 Theft of returned stock	*A lucrative side line* Partly damaged stock returned by customers to a building material manufacturer was removed from the warehouse by staff and sold to the public. The fraud was discovered when a customer informed the company that he had been offered their products at reduced prices.	• Poor control over unaccepted/incorrect loads, incorrect loads etc. • As for *Theft of inventory* above.
3 Theft of valuable scrap	*Valuable metal* The employee at a manufacturing company who was responsible for sending high quality scrap metal to another company for reprocessing colluded with an employee at the processing company to falsify the weights and types of	• As for *Theft of inventory* above.

Type of fraud	*Examples*	*Warning signs*
Management and employee frauds	metal sent for reprocessing. The profits from the 'lost' metal were shared between the two employees.	
4 Metering and weighbridge frauds	Employees at a bulk plaster supplier stole plaster and sold it for cash to the local building trade, splitting the proceeds among factory employees as a 'bonus'. The plaster was loaded onto lorries, weighed and appropriate delivery documentation produced. However, part of the load was unloaded at another warehouse used by the conspirators before it reached its destination. The fraud was not detected by the company's customers, who were small to medium-sized building contractors, because most did not have weighbridges and were content to have the plaster tipped into their silos or storage bins. They relied on the delivery note as confirmation of the quantity delivered. The nature of the product is that some is lost by spillage and exact yields on mixing with water are difficult to determine – where customers did query the quality of the product false explanations were given by employees concerning humidity variation or wastage at construction sites due to poorly skilled plasterers.	• Evidence of tampering with metering or weighbridge equipment, frequent breakdowns of such equipment. • No independent checks of such equipment on a regular basis. • Metering or weighbridge equipment becomes faulty at unusual times of the day or week. • Complaints from customers regarding poor quality or low yields (assuming such complaints are monitored independently).
5 Manipulation of inventory records	*Improving an earnout* During an earnout period the profit and loss account of a new subsidiary was closely monitored. Costs were falsely	• Unexplained differences between book and physical stock. • No analysis of stock lines,

capitalised to improve the subsidiary's results. Certain balance sheet accounts were seldom reviewed and the transfers were not detected. The total appeared to be small, but multiplied by the earnout factor, it was highly significant.

suppliers, customers, delivery drivers, warehouse staff involved in stock losses.

- Stock lines with long turnover periods.
- Abnormally large holdings of particular stock lines.
- Alterations to stocktake schedules or valuation working papers.
- Unusual number or value of credit notes or adjustments around period end or date of stocktake.
- Items held in suspense accounts.
- Stock purported to be located in unusual or inaccessible places.

CASH AND PAYMENT SYSTEMS

Management and employee frauds

1 Misuse of cheques and payment systems
2 Manipulation of bank reconciliations and cash books (*concealment devices*)

External frauds

3 Money transfer frauds
4 Forged cheques

Type of fraud	*Examples*	*Warning signs*
Management and employee frauds		
1 Misuse of cheques and payment systems	*Attempt to divert £23 million* A senior accounts assistant at an oil company conspired to defraud the company of £23 million. She and her lover, the director of an offshore based oil consultancy with an office in the same town, sought to divert an annual lease payment of £23 million, relating to an oil rig, to a bank account in Switzerland. The accounts assistant stole the form authorising the transfer of the funds and substituted an international payment application directing the money to the Swiss bank account. The manager of the Swiss bank had allegedly been paid a $500,000 bribe. The payment application was sent to the company's bank by post with a message on the top of the form urging the bank to make the payment on time. Her lover had planned to make it appear that a company in Abu Dhabi, with which he had been working on a joint venture, was doing very well and to bring back the funds to Aberdeen as profits from that venture. An employee at the company's bank queried the payment application when he saw the message written on the top of the form and alerted her employer. *Payable to the wife, using her maiden name* A company secretary allegedly misappropriated £19,000 by	• Controls over the final release of funds inadequate for the amounts involved (for example, only a check that the signatory is authorised to sign). • Processing of large payments performed by junior personnel. • Poor security over cheques, cheque books and returned cheques. • No clear desk policy. • Poor control over cheques and payment instructions between approval and processing. • Management override of normal approval procedures. • Last minute requests for payments, not supported by all the relevant documentation. • Abbreviated payee names. • Alterations to date, amount or

preparing a cheque in his capacity as company secretary and administrator of a pension fund. The cheque was drawn on a pension fund account and made payable to his wife using her maiden name. He arranged for the cheque to be signed by only one of the cheque signatories (when the other cheque signatories were away).

Cheque signing machines

A cash supervisor persuaded her assistant who held the second key to a cheque signing machine that it would be 'simpler' if she held both keys. The supervisor then produced a cheque with a blank payee, completing the payee details manually. The attempted fraud was fortunately picked up by the company's bankers.

No one will miss them

An employee took three cheques from the back of an unused cheque book. The employee then forged the signatures on the cheques, making them payable to a company which supplied goods to a private company owned by the employee. The supplier company was not a party to the fraud.

Colour photocopiers

An employee prepared a counterfeit cheque for £88,000 using a high quality multi-colour printer. The cheque incorporated the company's logo and all the other characteristics of the company's computer cheques except

payee; typed or handwritten details inserted on computer-generated cheques.

- Bank account through which cheque paid different to account number on standing data.
- Unusual arrangements with banks for authorisation of transactions.
- Valuable documents or documents containing authorising signatures left unattended.
- Weak procedures over the release of specimen signatures to banks.
- Poor security over cancelled cheques.
- Old or unidentified credits allowed to remain on ledger.
- No independent check on items going through suspense accounts.

Type of fraud	***Examples***	***Warning signs***
Management and employee frauds	that it had been completed on a typewriter. Close examination of the counterfeit cheque revealed that the signatures were photocopies. According to the company's records the cheque with the particular number of the counterfeit cheque had been cancelled. *Those dangling credits are a liability after all* The accounting function of a company's regional office was largely under the control of one person. The individual made unsupported cash advances to himself, using old unclaimed credit balances to conceal the debit entries. *A plan to free hostages* Two men sought to defraud a large company of £40 million. They set up bank accounts in its name in the Isle of Man, claiming to be representatives of the company, on the pretext that it was part of a covert operation to secure the release of its employees held as hostages held in the Middle East. A mole in the company was allegedly going to have diverted the funds out of the company. However, the manager at the bank in the Isle of Man became suspicious when they were told that large sums of money would be paid in by the company and taken out almost immediately.	

2 Manipulation of bank reconciliations and cash books

A roller coaster

The managing director of a company had incurred gambling debts which he was unable to pay off. He arranged for his company to make the payment by purchase of a bank draft. Since there were numerous transactions for the amount involved the improper payment, which had not been recorded in the accounting records, was matched in the reconciliation process with a genuine transaction of the same amount, leaving the reconciliation difference to appear as a proper item.

Outstanding lodgements . . .

An employee who was on sick leave did not collect his wages for four months. The cash was stolen by the cashier. She was also responsible for the preparation of bank reconciliations. The amounts of missing cash were shown as 'outstanding lodgements' on the bank reconciliation. The person reviewing the bank reconciliation did not notice the same items appearing on the bank reconciliations each month. The fraud was only picked up at year end.

Contras

Certain receipts into a bank nostro account were immediately paid out by letter of instruction rather than by cheque. No entry was made in the accounting records, but the entries on the statement were marked as 'contra'. The explanation given that these were bank errors corrected on the same day. In fact, the payments were being made to a director.

- No independent check of bank reconciliations – cursory review only.
- No independent check of bank reconciliations against cash books, original paying-in slips and ledger postings.
- Excessive numbers of contras and adjustments on reconciliations.
- No review of endorsements or alterations on returned cheques.

Type of fraud	***Examples***	***Warning signs***
Management and employee frauds	Subsequently, in another variation, entries were made in the books which merely debited and credited the cash book so that the entries in the bank statements could be matched to an accounting voucher and the books balanced but no entries had been made to the account of the remitter or of the recipient of the funds.	
	Missing cheques	
	Two cheques were extracted from a cheque book and made payable to an individual, in whose name a bank account had been previously opened to receive the cheques. The signature on the cheques was forged by copying authorised signatures from returned cheques. The cheques were entered in the cash book with the narrative 'missing cheques' against them so that cheques would not appear on the bank reconciliation as reconciling items.	
External frauds		
3 Money transfer frauds	For examples see *Misuse of money transfer systems* under *Other banking frauds.*	
4 Forged cheques	*Temporary staff handle cheques*	• As for *Misuse of cheques and payment systems* above.
	Two forged company cheques amounting to £40,000 were cleared through the central clearing system. The cheques	

were correct in every detail including the signatures and the magnetic strips. The serial numbers duplicated actual cheques issued by the company earlier in the same week. A temporary accounts assistant at the company had a boyfriend who was a member of a group of fraudsters who had carried out cheque frauds on a number of companies. In each case an accounts assistant was 'planted' at the company concerned to obtain the necessary information.

Taken to the cleaners

A group of fraudsters obtained details of the bank accounts of a number of companies. One of the conspirators ran a cleaning firm which had a contract to clean an office block where a number of the companies were located. Using the details obtained the fraudsters telephoned banks to obtain cheque books for the accounts.

The fraudsters then attempted to cash cheques amounting to approximately £1.4 million. They forged signatures copied from stolen company documents, provided bogus letters and paid in funds using cheques from other stolen cheque books. They sent attractive young women, recruited in nightclubs, to collect the cash, paying them off with a slice of the proceeds.

Lost copy of the authorised signature . . .

An individual allegedly sought to defraud two companies of £650,000 by falsely representing to their banks that they had authorised withdrawals from their accounts. On each occasion a bogus bank official rang the company saying

Type of fraud	**Examples**	**Warning signs**
External frauds	that the authorising signature had been lost, that a new one was required and that someone would call to collect it. The signature together with a compliments slip was picked up from the company's offices. Shortly afterwards, someone claiming to be the chief executive of the company called the bank asking to transfer an amount to accounts at other banks. A bank official realised that the call was fraudulent and did not agree to the request. When the premises of the fraudster were searched the names and telephone numbers of many companies and executives who had been called were found on papers stored in the roof space.	
	Covering up a fraud with a fraud An accountant at a small company raised a wages cheque for cash for £10,000, £2,000 being posted to the cash book. This was compensated by posting a receipt for certain miscellaneous sales (which were posted directly to the nominal ledger) at £8,000 less than the invoiced amount. The bank reconciliation therefore reconciled. The accountant was responsible for drawing cheques and preparing the bank reconciliation and there was little supervision of his work.	

OTHER FRAUDS

Management and employee frauds

1 Share support schemes
2 Insider dealing
3 Misuse of government grants/funding
4 Misuse of pension funds and other assets
5 Omitted contingencies
6 Company car scheme frauds
7 Payroll frauds
8 Misuse of intercompany and suspense accounts (*concealment devices*)

External frauds

9 Money laundering
10 Bogus curriculum vitae
11 Bogus insurance cover

Type of fraud	***Examples***	***Warning signs***
Management and employee frauds		
1 Share support schemes	*Sub-underwriting your own share issue* Two directors of a company allegedly paid for millions of pounds of shares in the company by laundering company funds through private offshore companies which they had set up. The company had recently bid for another company, the terms being six new shares for each share in the company being acquired, or cash. When the stock market crashed the shares in the acquiring company fell by about 60 per cent and the shareholders in the acquiree wanted cash rather than shares. As a result millions of shares had to be disposed of by the underwriters. One of the directors was a sub-underwriter, being responsible for shares valued at several millions of pounds. He paid for the shares using company funds.	• Volatile share price. • Company in perilous financial position or experiencing difficult trading conditions. • Key director (and shareholder) about to leave. • Any evidence of complex structures, involving offshore companies or countries with bank secrecy laws. • Imminent hostile bid or acquisition in volatile market conditions. • Defensive replies about particular transactions. Lack of openness. • Transactions/files handled exclusively by senior management. • Senior executives have large shareholding, living expensively and have borrowed heavily on shares of company.

2 Insider dealing

Getting out while the going is good

The chairman of a quoted company sold a large holding of his company's shares just before an announcement of worse than expected figures. Shortly afterwards the chairman resigned and trading in the company's shares was suspended. When trading resumed the shares traded at one-third of the original price. The chairman drew up a deed of gift, purporting to give his shares to his girlfriend – in fact he had authorised his bank to sell them after his resignation.

A church meeting

Two men, a journalist and his brother, an engineer, dealt in the shares of a quoted company ahead of a profits warning being issued. The company's group accountant and company secretary had divulged that a profits warning was imminent at a church meeting the previous day.

- Dealings in the company's shares by directors or others associated with the company immediately prior to a profits warning, an acquisition or takeover bid or other transaction which will affect the price of the company's shares.
- Rules regarding dealings in the company's shares not well known among staff or not applied in practice.

3 Misuse of government grants/funding

Government funding disappears

A manufacturing company received several million pounds of government grants and loans to develop a product. The money should have been paid to a second manufacturer who had been awarded the contract to develop the product. Instead, the managing director of the first company and the managing director and finance director of the second allegedly channelled the funds through a Panamanian-registered, Swiss-based company. The directors of the second company had set up several Swiss bank accounts.

- Company in perilous financial position or difficult trading conditions.
- Any evidence of complex structures, involving offshore companies or countries with bank secrecy laws.
- Transactions/ files handled exclusively by senior management.

Type of fraud	***Examples***	***Warning signs***
Management and employee frauds	Later the project was in effect funded a second time and on that occasion a direct payment was made from the first company to the second for the work carried out. However, the first company ran into financial difficulties the following year and receivers were appointed. The fraud was one of the factors which led to the collapse of the company.	• No clear accountability for government funding and loans.
4 Misuse of pension funds and other assets	*Bailing out a sinking ship* The chief executive of a construction company which was in financial difficulties allegedly stole a cheque for nearly £1 million and shares in various quoted companies from the group's pension fund.	• Employing company in a perilous financial position. • Access to assets created through legal arrangements, e.g., powers of attorney, investment management agreements, trustee companies. • Pension fund has different accounting period from employer. • Transfers of assets between the pension fund and the company where the market value cannot be easily ascertained.

5 Omitted contingencies

Taking profits early

A construction company normally took the profit on contracts when a completion certificate was issued. However, due to poor results on other contracts, the company wished to claim a particular contract as complete and provided a side letter to a customer, setting out certain undertakings in consideration for the issue of a completion certificate, thereby enabling profit to be taken on the contract even though certain contractual obligations had not been completed.

Further examples

Further examples of this type of fraud, in the financial sector, are set out under *Other banking frauds* below.

- Completions ahead of schedule or large number of and/or significant transactions close to the period end.
- Company in perilous financial position or difficult trading conditions.

6 Company car scheme frauds

Ex fleet cars going cheap

The manager of a company car scheme stole over 100 vehicles. Many were sold cheaply in secret to senior employees. None of the employees asked where the vehicles came from because they felt they had earned the bargains by hard work.

Secretary collects ex-fleet cars

The manager of a company car fleet was suspected of having sold company cars at less than their market value. In the previous eighteen months five company cars had been sold to the same secretary.

- No independent checks on the prices at which, and the parties to whom, company cars are sold.
- Same purchaser for range of models.
- Single source of supply for key services, e.g., repairs.

Type of fraud	***Examples***	***Warning signs***
Management and employee frauds **7 Payroll frauds**	*The phantom of the factory* A manager at a remote plant, where there was a large number of employees, was responsible for submitting time cards and summary sheets for employees. He input details for a dummy employee and submitted weekly time cards for the 'employee' over a three-year period. *Fraud related pay* The managing director of an overseas subsidiary pressurised staff into making unauthorised commission, bonus and overtime payments through the payroll. The monthly management accounts were manipulated by the managing director. The results were never investigated in detail by the parent company. *Not a man for the detail* The accountant at a company increased his salary by more than the percentage given to other staff. The accountant was responsible for preparing the salary increase sheets. Although the sheets were authorised by a senior official, the official did not check the underlying information.	• Remote locations where input is controlled by one person. • No independent check on bonuses, commissions and overtime payments. • Individual not on voters' register. • No zero-based budgeting. Rolling budgets.

Fraud	Example	Warning signs
8 Misuse of intercompany and suspense accounts	*An unreconciled account* The chairman of a company concealed payments for his own account by arranging for the payments to be debited in the holding company books in its intercompany account with a foreign subsidiary. No proper reconciliation of the accounts was performed, allowing the payments to go undetected for a considerable time.	• Intercompany accounts not reconciled and adjustment not posted (differences all treated as 'timing differences'). • Reasons for transactions, particularly with overseas companies, unclear, or shrouded in secrecy. • Large round sum cash movement.
	Payments to a director disguised Payments to a director were concealed by transferring funds to the account of a subsidiary then returning the funds to the holding company but recording the remittance as from an assumed name rather than from the subsidiary. The funds were then paid to the director on the grounds that the remittance had been for his account. The entries were all made through a contra account and not reviewed by the auditors.	
External frauds		
9 Money laundering	*A bogus property company* Drug traffickers importing cannabis from West Africa employed a solicitor who set up a client account. The solicitor deposited £500,000 received from them, later transferring the funds to his firm's bank account. Subsequently, acting on instructions, the solicitor withdrew the funds from the account and used them to purchase a number of properties on behalf of the drug traffickers.	• See separate appendix.

Type of fraud	***Examples***	***Warning signs***
External frauds	*Theft of company funds* The director of a wholesale supply company issued cheques to third parties which were deposited into their respective bank accounts, both in the United Kingdom and with offshore banks. Cheques drawn on the third party accounts were handed back to the director made payable to him personally and were paid into his personal bank account. False company invoices were raised purporting to show the supply of goods by third parties to the company.	
10 Bogus curriculum vitae	*The man for the job* An individual who had already served a four year prison sentence for obtaining property by deception obtained a job as marketing director of an organisation after submitting a bogus CV and references. His CV and references were so glittering that he was head-hunted to the position after he applied for, but failed to win, a less senior position. The CV stated that the individual had a triple honours MBA degree and that he was fluent in Mandarin, Chinese and Japanese. A glowing reference, apparently from a Home Office minister, was attached. In fact everything was bogus. Despite his complete lack of credentials for the job he managed to keep up the charade for almost four months before being found out.	• Grandiose claims or references from people in 'high places' which are 'too good to be true'. • Gaps in employment history not accounted for. • References not checked. • Details on CVs not independently verified. Failure to follow up discrepancies. • Any attempt at interview to mislead, extreme defensiveness, contradictory answers, vague replies.

A hat trick

A credit controller committed the same fraud, involving teeming and lading and manipulation of the aged debtors analysis, at three different companies over a period of 10 years. On further investigation it transpired that he had claimed on his CV to be a chartered accountant. In fact he had never taken any of the chartered accountant's exams and was not a member.

None of the three companies had checked the information on his CV. If they had done so, it might have put them on notice that there was something dubious about the employee. In fact he had a criminal record and the gaps in his employment history related, in part, to time spent in prison.

11 Bogus insurance cover

Not worth the paper it's written on

A company which offered extended insurance guarantees on electrical appliances defrauded a number of major companies of more than £6 million by issuing bogus insurance warranties. The company used photocopying machines to create bogus documents. They then passed these off as five-year extended insurance guarantees for electrical appliances. As a result the companies which used the extended warranties had to pick up the bill when their customers issued insurance claims. The director of the company led a life of luxury. He had a £250,000 farm in Sussex, a string of racehorses and ran two Rolls Royces.

- Quality of documentation below the standard expected.
- Unusually low insurance premiums.
- Intermediary ensures that all contact with the insurer is via him.

PUBLIC SECTOR – FURTHER EXAMPLES

Management and employee frauds

1 Underbilling/underringing
2 Kickbacks and inducements

External frauds

3 Substandard products
4 False claims for grants/benefits

Type of fraud	***Examples***	***Warning signs***
Management and employee frauds		
1 Underringing/underbilling	*A heavy toll* 18 men defrauded a local authority of £1 million over five years relating to tunnel tolls. Automatic collection was introduced in 1980 with drivers dropping cash into a computerised hopper. Until the transition was complete, toll collectors were given tickets to dispense to each motorist. If a driver did not take the ticket after depositing his cash the operator would pocket the toll and hand the ticket to the next car. Even when the computerised system had been fully introduced the fraudsters found a way of halting the communications between the computer and the counting room. One official earning £10,000 a year ran three cars and owned a boat and a caravan. The fraudsters together siphoned off about £11,000 a week. The fraud was uncovered when an anonymous letter was sent to the tunnel's management.	• See *Sales* above
2 Kickbacks and inducements	*A lucrative contract* Three managers from a public sector organisation took bribes from a garage owner worth hundreds of thousands of pounds including foreign holidays and cash in return for awarding road vehicle maintenance contracts. Over a five-year period, the officials were given dozens of gifts and	• See *Purchases* above

holidays. In return they sent vehicles from the 2000 strong road fleet to the garage to be maintained. Some of the maintenance was never carried out.

Double glazing commission

An environmental health officer passed lists of home owners applying for loan improvement grants to a double glazing salesman. He also recommended the salesman's company to householders. He was paid commission of £6,000 on contracts worth £156,000 over a 10-month period.

Cash, foreign holidays and call girls . . .

Eleven officials of a government agency received cash, foreign holidays, call girls, home improvements and clothing in return for handing out lucrative contracts to builders for the maintenance of royal palaces, laboratories, law courts and government offices.

A BMW and a holiday in Florida

The chief executive of a munitions company gave a BMW car and a holiday in Florida to an official as an inducement to show favour to his firm with regard to contracts to supply mortar ammunition.

Type of fraud	***Examples***	***Warning signs***
Management and employee frauds	*Brown envelopes* A company director and his general manager obtained contracts by bribing an official in a government department. They met the official at a London pub and gave him envelopes containing cash. In return the official authorised invoice payments for contracts that were not completed.	
External frauds **3 Substandard products**	*Garden rubbish fuels power station* Four directors of a company which was supposed to supply high-grade blended coal worth £36 per ton to a power station supplied inferior coal worth £4.60 per ton and, on occasion, garden rubbish. The individuals got away with the fraud because they bribed three power station samplers £1,200 a week. The conspiracy was discovered six months into the two-year contract when output from the power station dropped by 6 per cent due to the low quality fuel being burned.	• See *Purchases* above

4 False claims for grants/benefits

Charity begins at home

The director of a charity allegedly obtained grants from a council and government department. It was alleged that he bought a property in Barbados for his retirement. He paid salaries to his three daughters, his son and his wife and made payments to BUPA and paid domestic bills for his home in Surrey out of the charity's funds. The council investigated the charity's books and became suspicious when they saw a large bank overdraft and a number of 'unusual' invoices.

Bogus companies claim grants

An individual obtained £200,000 of regional development grants dishonestly. He formed three companies and claimed that he had created 79 new jobs. In fact the companies never operated. He got the 79 names at random from job centres together with the individuals' national insurance numbers. He also forged leases for premises which he said he was renting and 'borrowed' thousands of pounds worth of electronic equipment to show to an accountant before putting in his application for the grants.

The individual attempted to obtain the money in order to rescue another of his companies which was in financial difficulties. Staff at the grants office recognised one of the names as that of the individual's son.

Type of fraud	***Examples***	***Warning signs***
External frauds	*Pension allowance fraud* Six individuals ran a nationwide counterfeiting operation to obtain £3.6 million from social security by deception. Forged pension allowance books were used at post offices. The printing plates and forgeries were very professional.	
	Dr Invisible Two GPs lied about the numbers of doctors working in their practice in order to claim allowances and payments amounting to £100,000.	

LENDING

Management and employee frauds

1 Loans to fictitious borrowers
2 Use of nominee companies
3 Deposit transformation
4 Transactions with connected companies
5 Asset quality camouflage
6 Kickbacks and inducements
7 Use of parallel organisations
8 Funds transformation

External frauds

9 Impersonation and false information on loan applications
10 Double-pledging of collateral/land flips/forged or valueless collateral
11 Misappropriation of loan funds by agents/customers

Type of fraud	*Examples*	*Warning signs*
Management and employee frauds		
1 Loans to fictitious borrowers	*A busy bank manager* The branch manager of a well-known bank arranged fake loans amounting to £260,000 using 70 false names on bogus loan applications.	• No independent checks on identity or status of borrowers. • 'Thin' loan files. • Sketchy or non-existent financial information but management claim the 'creditworthiness of the borrower is undoubted'. • Borrowers with common or like-sounding names. • Photocopied documentation, missing details (e.g., phone number, VAT number on invoices/ letterheads). • Borrower not on voters' register, missing credit checks or references. • Valuations which seem high. Same valuer used extensively between various borrowers. • Commercial customers or sig-

nificant personal borrowers who are not generally known to staff.

- Loan funds paid away before all the necessary formalities have been completed.
- Remuneration closely linked to the number and/or value of new loans.
- Generous extensions or revised terms when the borrower defaults.
- Significant numbers of borrowers introduced by same source.

2 Use of nominee companies

'Customers' in sunny climates

A bank used a number of tax haven companies as nominees to receive the proceeds of certain fraudulent loans. The ownership of the companies was concealed through the use of trustee and management arrangements offered by local solicitors in the tax havens concerned. However, the same local solicitor was named as a director on many of the companies. This was a clue to the possible ownership of the companies.

- File not kept in main filing. Handled exclusively by a senior official.
- Evasive answers re particular loans. Unusual behaviour.
- Documentation which the directors say does not relate to the business, held in directors' offices or outside the main filing.
- 'Thin' loan files.

Type of fraud	Examples	Warning signs
Management and employee frauds	*Personal papers* The managing director of a bank made a loan to himself via an offshore company owned by him. The loan file gave no indication that the company was owned by him. It suggested that the company was owned by one of his contacts overseas and that the managing director had merely introduced the business. The file indicated that the loan was to meet short-term working capital requirements. However, there was very little information on file about the company, its directors, its activities or financial position.	• Sketchy or non-existent financial information. • Loans to offshore companies with no clear business purpose. • Complex structures shrouded in secrecy. • Few details about the people behind the borrower company. • Loan given on the basis of a strong personal recommendation of a senior official but few other details on file. • Vague wording re the reason for the loan, the source of the contact or the nature of relationship. • Like sounding names/common links between various borrowers or with any of the directors or companies connected with them.

3 Deposit transformation

A loan at one remove

A bank placed a deposit with another bank and used it as security against a loan by that bank to nominated beneficiaries. No record was made of the pledge or of the contingent liability arising in respect of the ultimate loan, thereby concealing not only the credit exposure but also retaining the benefit of the deposit to satisfy liquidity reporting requirements.

An unusual strategy

A bank with liquidity problems made substantial medium-term deposits with a disreputable bank when the funds were urgently required to meet pressing commitments. It transpired that the deposits had been used by the bank concerned to secure lending to a company related to the directors.

- Pledges over deposits (disclosed by audit confirmations which have specifically requested such pledges to be disclosed).
- Deposits continually rolled over.
- Long-term deposits held when liquidity is tight.
- Unusual counterparties.
- Documentation or files held in directors' offices outside main filing.
- Evasive replies when access to such documents is requested.
- Weak controls re the giving and recording of guarantees.

4 Transactions with connected companies

An attractive lending opportunity

The chief executive of a bank approved a loan to a company relating to the development of a golf course and country club. As part of the deal for obtaining the loan he entered into a secret joint venture agreement to be paid 30 per cent of the profit from the venture. The profit was paid into a private company in which he and the other associates involved in the project were shareholders. All the files relating to the joint venture were kept in the chief

- As for *Loans to fictitious borrowers* and *Use of nominee companies* above.
- Loan goes into arrears after a short time.
- Jottings on file which are not consistent with other information or file (e.g., names,

Type of fraud	*Examples*	*Warning signs*
Management and employee frauds	executive's office. There was no indication of the joint venture on the main loan file.	addresses, telephone numbers of unknown individuals). • Repayments made by persons other than the borrower.
5 Asset quality camouflage	*Hidden stakes* A director of a bank approved a loan to an offshore company in order for the company to purchase shares in a public company. A sharp increase in the share price was predicted. A director of the bank and the finance director of the company were joint shareholders of the offshore company. The bank director's shareholding in the offshore company was not disclosed to his fellow directors. The anticipated increase in the share price did not occur. Subsequently the finance director of the public company defaulted on the loan repayments. The director of the bank made a number of repayments on his behalf via another offshore company owned by him so that the loan did not come under scrutiny by his fellow directors or the auditors. *Large exposures* The chief executive of a bank agreed with a particular borrower that the finance for a series of large projects overseas should be spread between a number of offshore companies. The ownership of the companies was carefully	• As for *Use of nominee companies* and *Funds transformation*

disguised so that the true extent of the borrowing to the customer was concealed from the auditors and the regulator. Certain of the projects ran into difficulties. The complex structure enabled advances to be made in respect of apparently new, unconnected ventures to meet loan repayments on the ventures which were in difficulties.

6 Kickbacks and inducements

Brown envelopes

The lending officer at a bank took bribes from customers in return for granting loans. The borrowers would not normally have been able to obtain credit from the institution concerned. The loan officer falsified details regarding the financial status of the borrowers so that the loan applications appeared to meet the bank's lending criteria.

- Remuneration closely linked to number or value of new loans.
- Excessive amounts of business generated by particular loan officers.
- Lending criteria overridden regularly by particular loan officers.
- Sole contact customers.
- Change in pattern of business towards high risk area.
- Concentration of lending in particular sector or through particular sources of introduction.
- Strong personal recommendation of a director or lending officer but missing data or documentation.

Type of fraud	*Examples*	*Warning signs*
Management and employee frauds		
7 Use of parallel organisations	*Passing the parcel* A bank purchased loans from a parallel bank (ultimately under common ownership) before its year end in exchange for an unrecorded arrangement whereby the parallel bank would repurchase the loans at face value after its year end. In order to conceal the transaction from the head office auditors, these loans were transferred to a subsidiary which was given unrecorded guarantees to support the loans. *Transforming deposits* The branch manager of a bank dealt personally with certain depositors and their accounts, when these would normally have been managed by more junior members of staff. It transpired that the manager was assisting the depositors to launder funds through overseas branches of the bank, returning them to the home country represented as deposits by non-residents on which interest was treated as non-taxable. *Pressing personal needs* A bank made a short-term loan to an individual overseas. The reason for the loan was to meet 'pressing personal needs'. In fact the individual was a friend of the managing director. The individual had incurred significant gambling	• As for *Use of nominee companies* and *Funds transformation* above. • Apparent repayment of problem loans shortly before the period end. • Unexpected new lending close to the period end. • Transfers of loans from companies which may be under common ownership or with which there may be other links. • Poor controls re the giving and recording of guarantees or similar commitments. • Transactions or structures shrouded in secrecy. • Change in pattern of business with related organisations.

debts which he was unable to repay. The loan was fully secured against a cash deposit recorded in the name of an offshore company, ostensibly owned by an associate of the individual. In fact the offshore company was owned by the managing director of the bank and the funds deposited were the bank's own money, routed into the account via a series of complex transactions. The borrower subsequently defaulted on the loan.

8 Funds transformation

Round the houses

A bank made a loan relating to a property development undertaken by the chairman's brother-in-law. There was a shortfall in the value of the security held for the loan and the loan was non-performing. To avoid making a provision the bank transferred an amount equal to the shortfall through a branch, subsidiary and an associated institution under its management and returned the funds to the bank as though they were a receipt from the chairman's brother-in-law.

- Source of receipt not consistent with standing data (especially after a period of non-payment).
- Loan becomes current shortly before the period end or shortly before an audit visit.
- Transactions with other companies in the group or with associates where the business reason is unclear.
- Any evidence of transactions with 'parallel organisations' in particular offshore companies and companies in countries with bank secrecy laws.

Type of fraud	***Examples***	***Warning signs***
Management and employee frauds		• Annotations on file which do not appear to relate to the borrower (e.g., names, telephone numbers and other jottings). • File not kept in main filing.
External frauds		
9 Impersonation and false information on loan applications	*'Mr Money'* An undischarged bankrupt and convicted fraudster entertained the branch manager of a well-known bank at Claridges and the Cup Final. The man posed as an international lawyer and a duke. 25 bank accounts were opened for the man, nicknamed Mr Money. When the overdraft facilities were exhausted, Mr Money loaded his Rolls Royce with art treasures and fled to his chateau in France. *A casting error* A customer submitted false accounts to a bank when renegotiating its overdraft facilities. The audited accounts had been altered. The customer went to great lengths to make the accounts appear genuine. Unfortunately, the customer did not cover his tracks completely – the source and application of funds statement did not cast.	• Grandiose claims or personal details. • Lavish entertaining of bank personnel or evidence of an extravagant lifestyle. • No personal visits or on-site appraisal of the customer or his business. • Business ventures that are 'too good to be true'. • Sole contact customers. • Difficulty in corroborating the borrower's credentials or status. • Inconsistent or missing documentation, inaccuracies or alterations.

You can prove anything with computers

Two directors of a large toy manufacturing company secured bank and other loans amounting to £8 million for their ailing company. They used fake computer records of sales to convince the banks and finance companies to lend them the money.

- No independent contact with or appraisal of referees or professionals giving comfort on the borrower.
- Inconsistencies in personal details when checked with independent sources (such as voter's register, credit status checks, etc).

External frauds

10 Double-pledging of collateral/land flips/forged or valueless collateral

A development in Docklands

Seven people connected with a redevelopment in Docklands, including estate agents and solicitors, allegedly arranged for the initial buyers of flats which were being built to resell their properties to various offshore companies at false market valuations. An overseas bank lent to new buyers on the basis of these valuations.

Bogus share certificates

Three businessmen allegedly attempted to defraud one of the major clearing banks of £3 million by using forged share certificates, supposedly worth £7 million, as collateral for a loan.

- As for *Impersonation/false information on loan applications* above.
- Valuer from outside the area in which the property is situated.
- Same valuer used on a large number of transactions.
- Same valuer used by both parties.
- Series of sales of particular assets over a short period with values increasing on each sale.
- Identity of principals difficult to ascertain/use of nominee or 'front' companies.

Type of fraud	*Examples*	*Warning signs*
		• Borrower known to have access to substantial assets (for example, pension fund assets) of a type similar to those pledged.
External frauds		
11 Misappropriation of loan funds by agents/ customers	*Appearances can be deceptive* A number of banks were allegedly defrauded by two individuals who tricked the banks into believing that they were providing short-term loans to fund international trade whereas the cash was going in long-term loans to two bankrupt West German companies. The banks were shown bogus bills and letters to convince them that the loans were for international trade. *A bridge too far* A solicitor obtained over £250,000 from a bank pretending the money was for the use of clients buying property. The solicitor asked the clients to sign blank forms in case bridging loans were required in a hurry. The solicitor had an arrangement with the bank that when bridging loans were required the money would be transferred into his firm's account. However, the money was not used for bridging	• As for *Impersonation/false information on loan applications* above.

loans but was instead used to top up his firm's own resources and to fund the solicitor's lifestyle of exotic holidays and lavish entertaining.

DEPOSIT TAKING

Management and employee frauds

1 Depositors' camouflage
2 Unrecorded deposits
3 Misuse of customer deposits/investments

External frauds

4 Money laundering
5 Fradulent instructions

Type of fraud	*Examples*	*Warning signs*
Management and employee frauds		
1 Depositors' camouflage	*The MD in disguise* Several depositor accounts at an overseas bank were in fact those of the managing director and principal shareholder. Some of the accounts had like-sounding names. Many others were offshore companies owned by the managing director.	• Similar or like-sounding names across various accounts. • Off-shore company depositors with no clearly defined business purpose or about which there are few details. • Customer resident in or has some connection with overseas jurisdictions associated with drugs trafficking, terrorism, etc.
2 Unrecorded deposits	*Deposits re-routed to fund personal activities* A director of an overseas bank took deposits from certain overseas customers into code-numbered accounts in a Swiss bank. He had the sole contact with most of the customers. Most of the customers wished to hold the funds on a long-term basis outside their country of residence. There was rarely any movement on the accounts. In fact most of the code-numbered accounts were personal accounts of the director. The funds were moved from there into other offshore companies of the director to finance various activities of a speculative nature in which he	• Evidence of deposit taking by any other company of which there are details on the premises, whether part of the regulated group or not. • Documentation held in directors' offices, outside main filing, which it is claimed have no connection with the business of the bank. • Evasive replies regarding such documents.

was engaged. The deposits were never recorded in the books of the bank.

3 Misuse of customer deposits/investments

Gambling with a customer's money

The branch manager of an overseas bank stole £730,000 from a customer's account over a two year period. He used the funds for gambling. The customer was a foreign resident who had been 'detained' by authorities overseas. The customer had appointed the manager as custodian of the funds during his period of detention. The manager was authorised to make withdrawals to purchase investments. In fact the manager used the customer's period of detention to steal from his account.

- Accounts where the funds or investments are held on a long-term basis with no regular contact with customer.
- Sole contact customers.
- No independent resolution of customer complaints.
- No independent review of the operation of hold mail accounts.

External frauds

4 Money laundering

Drugs money in disguise

Cash collected in the United States from street sales of drugs was smuggled across the border to Canada. The money was taken to currency exchanges to increase denomination of notes and reduce the bulk. Couriers were organised to hand carry the cash by air to London where it was paid into a branch of a Jersey-based financial institution. The money was then transferred to 14 accounts opened in company names, using local nominee directors, at the institution in Jersey.

- See examples of suspicious transactions at the back of this guide.

Type of fraud	***Examples***	***Warning signs***
External frauds	The funds were repatriated to North America in the form of loans to offshore property companies owned by the principals either using the Jersey deposits as collateral or by simply transferring the money back to North America. *Cocaine Charlie* A non-account holder used a branch to remit cash to Peru. Then, having opened an account, he regularly deposited a few thousand pounds in cash. There was no explanation of the origin of the funds. Following a disclosure to the National Drugs Intelligence Unit he was identified as having previously been suspected of cocaine dealing. It became clear that his business would not have generated the substantial wealth which the customer displayed and that his account was being used to purchase chemicals known to be used in the refining of cocaine. *Little and often* A customer held two accounts at branches of the same financial institution in the same area. Although he was unemployed it was noted that he deposited £500-£600 in cash every other day. It was established that he held a third account and had placed several thousand pounds on	

deposit in Jersey. As a result of these investigations, he was arrested and later convicted for offences related to the supply of drugs.

5 Fraudulent instructions

See *Other banking frauds*.

OTHER BANKING FRAUDS

Management and employee frauds

1 Dealing fraud
2 Omitted contingencies
3 Passing through (*concealment device*)
4 Rolling matching (*concealment device*)
5 Diverted postings (*concealment device*)
6 Misuse of volume accounts

External frauds

7 Cross firing (or 'cheque kiting')
8 Cheque frauds/new account frauds
9 Misuse of money transfer systems
10 Advance fee fraud
11 Credit card fraud

Type of fraud	***Examples***	***Warning signs***
Management and employee frauds		
1 Dealing fraud	*Everyone seems to make a profit* A dealer at an institution bought a particular security at 100. He then sold the shares to an investor at 101, when the market price was 103. The investor then sold the shares at 103 to another institution which in turn sold them on at a small profit to the first institution. Part of the profit made by the investor was paid as a kickback to the dealer at the first institution. *Heads I win, tales I win* The head of foreign exchange at a bank and his assistant helped an investor to earn 'profits' of approximately £0.5 million. The investor was given a margin trading account, allowing him to deal in foreign exchange. A deposit of about £130,000 was required. The investor had a 96 per cent success rate on his deals compared to a usual average of about 60 per cent. Details of the transactions were recorded on a trading sheet. Then the initial pencil entries were erased or other entries were written over them in ink. The deals were 'back-booked' – i.e., the element of risk was removed by entering the known results on the trading sheets instead of the speculated figures. A profit of about $3,000 was made on each transaction and these profits were deducted at the end of the day's trading when the	• Dealing book not marked to market on a daily basis. • Unusual levels of activity with particular counterparties. • Poor supervision in the dealing room. • Unusual trends in dealers' positions. • Significant number of unmatched deals in particular dealing books or with particular counterparties. • Significant number of cancelled deals. • Dealing books which are trading close to their limit. • No time stamping of deal tickets. • Abnormal profits or losses by particular dealers or certain of their clients.

bank was calculating its daily profit. A member of senior management became suspicious when the head of foreign exchange asked for another margin trading account to be opened.

A loophole in the program

In a foreign exchange dealing operation dealers input transaction details direct into the front office computer system. The back office obtained confirmation of all transactions by telephone from counterparties on the same day and re-input details into the computer. The computer would process only transactions which matched in all specified fields.

However, although trade dates were input by both the dealers and the back office, the comparison of these fields had been omitted in programming and as a result a loophole was created which allowed the dealers to misrepresent positions by recording them on other than their actual trade dates.

The markets didn't obey me . . .

An interest rate options dealer at a bank manipulated revaluation rates to hide an unrealised loss of £3 million, because the market had moved against him. Trading in interest rate options had commenced at the bank before back-office procedures were fully in place. In particular there was no facility for the back-office to check the valuation of interest rate options independently.

- Alterations on dealing sheets and related documentation.
- No daily reconciliation between dealers' profit and accounting profit.
- No independent checks on prices at which deals are done or on revaluations.
- Accounting procedures and controls lag seriously behind the introduction of new products.
- Discrepancies in trade dates between front and back office or with counterparties.

Type of fraud	***Examples***	***Warning signs***
Management and employee frauds	*No questions asked* A highly successful foreign exchange dealer, whose remuneration was linked closely to dealing profits earned, took unauthorised overnight positions in forward foreign exchange contracts. He booked the unauthorised deals the following day shortly before booking the deals which reversed the positions. Having made significant profits, on one occasion the markets in New York and Tokyo moved against him overnight. He doubled up his positions assuming the market would continue in the same direction. However the market reversed. The unauthorised activity was not picked up because the back office focused almost exclusively on checking settlement details on incoming confirmations ignoring trade dates and other details. Also details relating to forward deals were only checked as they reached settlement date. No questions were asked how the dealer managed to achieve a high level of profits despite a strategy where only very limited overnight positions were permitted.	
2 Omitted contingencies	*Side deal* The chairman and principal shareholder of a bank, who also owned and was a director of a bank overseas, gave a guarantee in the name of the bank to a customer of the overseas bank. The management of the bank were unaware that the guarantee had been given.	• Evidence of guarantee fees or telex messages to counterparties with whom the bank does not normally deal. • Any evidence that transactions are entered into by directors or

False guarantees

The vice-president of the London branch of an overseas bank conspired with a business consultant to defraud the bank by issuing guarantees to certain investors without the bank's knowledge. He claimed that he was acting on behalf of the bank.

senior management overriding normal procedures.

- Weak controls re the giving and recording of guarantees.

3 Passing through

Taking a cut

Certain Swiss banks paid commissions to another bank for the introduction of substantial client funds for discretionary management. The directors who had arranged the introduction believed that they personally rather than the bank should benefit from the commissions and, with management collusion, the commissions were paid away on receipt to personal accounts of the directors. Neither receipts or payments through the correspondent accounts were recorded.

- Absence of usual introduction fees.
- Usual business terms waived.
- Sole contact customers.
- Independent review of particular accounts is resisted.
- Contra items on nostro reconciliations.

4 Rolling matching

A roller coaster

An improper payment was matched in a nostro reconciliation with a genuine transaction for the same amount, which made it appear that the reconciling item related to a genuine transaction.

See also examples under *Cash and payment systems*.

- No independent one-for-one check of reconciliations and related documentation on a regular basis – cursory review only.
- Excessive numbers of contras and adjustments.

Type of fraud	*Examples*	*Warning signs*
Management and employee frauds		
5 Diverted postings	*Reciprocal arrangements* A bank facilitated fraudulent claims for export credits for certain customers. These customers placed funds in an overseas branch which then issued a letter of credit ostensibly for the purchase of export goods from the customers' businesses in the home territory. No export transactions actually took place but the funds were transferred to the home country, represented to the authorities as receipts for exports. Very substantial subsidies were claimed. In consideration for making these arrangements the general manager of the bank obtained the customers' agreement to use their current accounts with the bank to accept debits both for advances to parties related to the general manager and for transactions in breach of statutory credit limits.	• Unusual terms or activity on particular accounts. • Any evidence that a bank is actively involved in helping persons in other jurisdictions to break local laws.
6 Misuse of volume accounts	*Pro-rata fraud* The management of a bank charged amounts each month to interest expense crediting the equivalent amount to their own current accounts. To avoid detection exact amounts, calculated by reference to the total deposit liabilities on a day-to-day basis, were charged so that the correlation	• No independent review of personal accounts. • No independent review of interest rates charged to particular accounts. • Rates or terms of business

	between interest expense and deposit liabilities was maintained.	which do not conform to clearly documented policies approved by the board.
	The favoured few The managing director and principal shareholder of a bank arranged for all accounts relating to himself, his companies and accounts owned by all his relatives to be given a favourable rate of interest.	• Journals and adjustments posted to volume accounts which are not adequately explained.
External frauds		
7 Cross firing ('cheque kiting')	Cross firing is a fraud whereby a large balance in one or more bank accounts is built up, based on uncollected cheques drawn on similar accounts at other banks. The fraud often involves a multiplicity of such accounts the aim being to increase artificially a company's cash reserves or to decrease its cost of funding.	• Many deposits of similar and/or round sum amounts. • High proportion of transactions with another bank. • Deposits soon withdrawn. • Flow through account does not seem to have a business rationale. • Low average balance, high volume.
8 Cheque frauds/new account frauds	*The wonders of modern photocopiers* Four individuals made near perfect copies of stolen blank cheques on a stolen £20,000 Canon laser photocopier. They paid the bogus cheques into bank accounts under false names before withdrawing money from cash points.	• Alterations to cheques, etc. • Illegible signatures. • Inconsistencies in printing.

Type of fraud	Examples	Warning signs
External frauds	During a period of six months they printed £100,000 worth of cheques in a lock-up garage, cashed nearly half and stole a further £60,000 in a series of thefts and burglaries. The photocopies were so accurate that only forensic tests distinguished them from the real thing. *219 false bank accounts* Two individuals used false names to open 219 accounts across the country. They gave addresses taken from voters' registers and asked for cheque books and cheque guarantee cards to be sent to them. They then had the mail redirected by the Post Office on the pretext of moving house. The individuals used five accommodation addresses which ended up at a collection point in Slough. The individuals used a mobile office, with a filofax and a card index system to keep track of their transactions. A Post Office clerk recognised an address used by the individuals and alerted investigators because she knew the people who really lived there. The police then undertook a surveillance operation.	• Customer resident outside the bank's normal trading area. • Undue haste to open account. • Unusual appearance or behaviour of applicant. Extreme nervousness. • Any inconsistencies arising from normal status checks. Cheque and new account frauds are widespread in the retail banking sector and most large banks have specialist units to deal with such frauds.
9 Misuse of money transfer systems	*Unauthorised use of SWIFT codes* Six people allegedly attempted to defraud a bank. It was alleged that the money was transferred after correct codes and procedures authorising the transaction were received	• Control over final release of funds insufficient for the amounts involved – e.g., checking only that the signatory is authorised to sign.

by the bank in London enabling a message to be sent on the SWIFT system to a bank in Switzerland.

None of the individuals charged was an employee of the bank and the fraud attempts were not made by hacking into the bank's computer. No money was lost as the fraud was detected in time. The fraud was discovered by accident during a manual check of transactions after a computer breakdown.

Unauthorised use of passwords/codes to transfer securities

Two individuals conspired to defraud an international securities firm by making an unauthorised transfer of Eurobonds worth £5 million. One of the individuals, who worked at the securities firm, had access to computer passwords and codes. His associate had brought him into contact with a gang of international fraudsters who wanted him to move the bonds to an account in Switzerland. The bonds were later to be sold to dealers through unsuspecting businessmen. An employee of the securities firm spotted the illegal transfer shortly before the sale date.

Forged fax messages

A dealer forged fax messages from a US financial institution which enabled him to trade on the futures market as though he was an agent. When the futures the dealer had invested in were settled, the bankers he dealt through were left with a loss of £6 million.

- Transfers to or from accounts in offshore locations or countries with bank secrecy laws.
- Transfer to/from individuals who are not regular customers.
- Abbreviated payee names.
- Alterations to date, amount, payee.
- Weak control over documents between approval and processing.
- Processing of significant transactions performed by junior personnel.
- Poor security over room where transfers are made and over codes and passwords.
- No clean desk policy.

Type of fraud	***Examples***	***Warning signs***
External frauds	*Put in the pile for processing* Instructions by a bank to make international payments were transmitted from a department which had no other duties. Instructions were given to the department on a form signed by two authorised signatories and brought to the department by an internal messenger. The controls were, therefore, in principle, strong and effective. Outside fraudsters obtained a copy of the form (probably by bribing a cleaner), produced a forgery containing instructions to make very large payments to certain overseas banks (but ensuring the payments were well within the scale of the bank's normal payments) and arranged for the forgery to be left in the pile of outstanding instructions. The instructions were acted upon in the normal way.	
10 Advance fee fraud	*For a small fee* A lawyer was involved in a worldwide fraud in which people lost millions of pounds. He claimed to represent an overseas financial services firm and took fees to secure loans on favourable terms. The loans never materialised.	• See *Purchases* above.

11 Credit card fraud

Credit card frauds are often carried out by highly organised groups of fraudsters. Most credit card companies have taken sophisticated measures to counter such frauds. Detailed consideration of these frauds is outside the scope of this book.

INVESTMENT BUSINESS

Management and employee frauds

1 Bogus investments
2 Trading without authorisation
3 Selling client investments without authority
4 Dealing fraud
5 Share ramping
6 Insider dealing
7 Churning
8 Other management and employee frauds

External frauds

9 Money laundering
10 Bogus documents/stolen share certificates
11 Fraudulent instructions

Type of fraud	***Examples***	***Warning signs***
Management and employee frauds		
1 Bogus investments	*All that glitters is not a gilt* The directors of an investment management firm defrauded thousands of small investors. The firm promised the investors that the money would be invested in gilt-edged securities. When the firm collapsed there should have been more than £115 million invested in gilts whereas there was just £1.9 million. The investors' money had been invested in various highly speculative schemes resulting in losses of over £40 million. The money was also used to fund a lavish lifestyle and to buy properties, yachts, jets and luxury cars. The small investors, mainly elderly people, were taken in by glossy brochures and advertising, that their money was secure in gilt-edged stock. The company was run from plush, computerised offices. The firm offered portfolios which, it claimed, attracted lower capital gains tax rather than higher income tax and guaranteed a minimum monthly return. The firm paid any returns of capital expected by clients from new money invested by other clients. *Undermining the Poll Tax* An individual made £1.25 million by selling shares in a Cornish tin mining company. He sold £1.50 shares in his	• Products 'too good to be true' – for example, low risk high return products. • Glossy advertising/high pressure sales techniques combined with a vulnerable and inexperienced client base. • Explanation of transactions is complex or investments are in companies based on one-off ventures or promoting some 'miracle' product. • Abnormal levels of growth in profitability or margins achieved. • Documentation held in directors' offices which it is claimed have no connection with the business. • Complex accounting arrangements, over use of intermediaries, companies in offshore locations, or other

Royal Cornish Consuls United Tin Mining Cost Book Company and told shareholders that they were exempt from the Poll Tax under an ancient tin-mining charter.

An anagram for offshore

The director of an investment management company told clients that he was investing their money in offshore trusts, promising returns varying between 21 and 100 per cent a year. He actually spent the money on a system of horse-race betting. His impeccable social connections and personal charm led investors to trust him. Investors inquiring about their money were told it was 'offshore' – a mixture, according to the fraudster, of 'off' and an anagram of 'horse'.

The individual was at the same time employed as a public relations officer at a firm of accountants on £24,000 a year. No one at this firm or his own company became suspicious about the fact that he lived in a £500,000 house, had three children at private schools and held lavish parties. He spoke a great deal about his private means and an annuity he had.

The miracle cure

Three businessmen defrauded investors of £700,000. Investors bought bogus shares in a company which, they were told, had invested in a method of detecting salmonella and listeria bacteria.

factors which make it difficult to trace the movement of funds or investments.

Type of fraud	***Examples***	***Warning signs***
Management and employee frauds	*A paper chase* A commodity company gave the impression that it invested clients' funds properly. In fact the funds were not invested in commodities at all and the cash was received into the company's own bank account by the fraudsters. The fraudsters went to great lengths to generate internal documentation, accounting records and statements for clients. Management was also in collusion with third parties who helped them to cover up the fraudulent transactions including the return of third party 'confirmations' to the auditors. *Three Rolls Royces, a boat and a gambling habit* The director of a small investment consultancy persuaded more than 100 people to invest £1.75 million purportedly in fixed-term guaranteed-income bonds paying 14-18 per cent interest. In fact, the funds were not invested at all save in his own bank account. He paid investors the interest and capital they were due from new funds received from other investors. The investors were mainly elderly people who had invested their life savings or redundant people investing redundancy pay-offs. The individual used the money to fund an extravagant lifestyle. He had three Rolls Royces	

(and had a fourth on order at the time of his arrest), a boat and he gambled heavily.

All that glitters . . .

The director of an investment company falsely misrepresented to his clients that their funds would be invested in government securities. He produced valuation statements showing securities purchased which were false. He also forged gilts stock notes from a stockbroker. He also failed to keep proper accounts, produced accounts which failed to give a true and fair view and submitted false annual returns.

Bogus life insurance and pension policies

A director of a financial services company diverted investors' money into high risk investments, issuing clients with bogus life insurance and pension policies. He also stole funds from clients.

All that glitters is not a US Treasury Bond

A financier defrauded investors of £2.5 million. Clients thought that their money was invested in safe US Treasury Bonds. In fact the money was used to fund a lavish lifestyle. The financier brought three Rolls Royces, had a £500,000 house and held flamboyant parties.

Tied agents steal £4.7 million

Four directors of a firm of financial advisors, who were tied

Type of fraud	***Examples***	***Warning signs***
Management and employee frauds	agents of a life insurance subsidiary owned by a major bank, misappropriated £4.7 million of clients' funds. They defrauded about 400 investors by falsely representing that their firm managed their investments efficiently and honestly. They also persuaded customers to invest in a high interest account which never existed.	
2 Trading without authorisation	*Clients' money used to fund stock market losses* Two individuals used over £100,000 of clients' money to fund personal losses made on the stock market. The individuals had failed to provide proper details to the regulator to allow them to be authorised under the Financial Services Act but had continued to tell clients that they were authorised.	• New business developments where detailed advice has not been sought concerning the regulatory implications. • Tight liquidity position. • Unusual trends. • Reasons for transactions with suspected related parties unclear.
3 Selling client investments without authority	*Investment adviser cashes in client policies* An investment adviser sold clients' endowment policies, single premium bonds and investment bonds. His clients were mainly retired people of modest means. In many cases, he forged his clients' signatures and surrendered their policies without their consent. The investment adviser gambled away £1.6 million of his clients' money in an	• Abnormal levels of client sales, policy surrenders or unexpected departures from agreed investment strategies. • Evidence of significant personal dealing. • Missing documentation or

attempt to recoup stock market losses incurred during 1987.

authority letters or unusual aspects on client files.

4 Dealing frauds

See *Dealing frauds* under *Banking* above

5 Share ramping

The Panamanian bubble

The managing director of a financial services company acted as a financial adviser to a number of small quoted companies. He used a Panamanian company to buy on credit 4 million of the 7 million shares available in a particular company at inflated prices, thus giving a false impression of their value. His 'share ramping' activity eventually led to a loss of £3.4 million and the collapse of his firm. A well-known bank also lost money when they lent over £1 million to the financial services company secured on the company's shares.

- Abnormal increases in the prices of shares of companies for which the company acts as adviser or sponsor.
- Loans made or transactions, the commercial purpose of which is unclear.
- Complex structures/transactions with offshore or 'front' companies.

6 Insider dealing

Ahead of the markets

An employee of a financial services group allegedly dealt in the shares of a quoted company based on inside information obtained from a director of the company for whom he managed a share portfolio. The share dealings allegedly took place just before the quoted company announced that it had received a takeover bid.

- See *Insider dealing* under *Other Frauds* above.

Type of fraud	*Examples*	*Warning signs*
Management and employee frauds	*Making a quick buck* A management consultant, who had been asked by an insurance company to devise an incentive scheme to ensure that senior executives of a company which it was due to purchase would stay on after the takeover, bought shares in the company shortly afterwards and sold them on at a 50 per cent profit three weeks later.	
7 Churning	Churning involves the buying and selling of securities without the clients' knowledge to generate commission.	• Unusually high levels of activity on particular clients or high commission levels for particular clients or brokers. • Apparent departures from agreed investment strategy. • Client is rarely in contact with broker – for example, abroad for long periods.
8 Other management and employee frauds	*Fictitious clients* A 'half commission' dealer allegedly used various false names on dealing slips and contract notes to generate commission.	

	Back office fraud An employee in an investment business presented cheques for signature purporting to be payments of investment sale proceeds to clients. The payee was always a bank. The employee subsequently added his own bank account number to the payee names. The company did not produce a reconciliation of cash held and clients' balances so the fraud remained undetected for several months.	
	Stolen share certificates An individual stole share certificates while working as a transfers manager in a London stockbroker. He used the stolen share certificates to obtain a £60,000 loan from a bank.	
External frauds		
9 Money laundering	See main text.	• See main text.
10 Bogus documents/stolen share certificates	*Stolen share certificates* Three individuals conspired to defraud banks, stockbrokers and financial institutions of £12.5 million by inducing them to accept stolen share certificates. They tried to sell the shares, which had been stolen from one of the major securities firms, through another broker. They also tried to raise loans using the stolen shares as security. An employee at a stockbroking firm noticed that the signatures on the share transfer forms were forgeries.	• Weak physical security procedures. • Overdue reconciliations of custody records to securities held on the premises or to other depositaries.

Type of fraud	*Examples*	*Warning signs*
Management and employee frauds		• Significant number of items on reconciliations which cannot be explained. • Insufficient resources or inexperienced staff allocated to safe custody activities.
11 Fraudulent instructions	*Forged power of attorney* Two individuals allegedly plotted to obtain shares from a bank. The bank held the shares on behalf of one of the individual's great aunt. It was alleged that he flew to his great aunt's villa abroad and obtained a specimen signature. A letter was then forged saying that he had power of attorney for her. The letter was used in an attempt to obtain the shares. However, a bank employee who had handled the account for 30 years spotted the attempted fraud and called the police. The police found a list of sample signatures and a word processor at the individual's home which was used to print the letters to the bank.	• Instructions out of line with client's usual activities. • Abnormal haste to complete the transaction. • Unusual aspects in documentation, for example, small differences in letterheads, paper used, typescript, handwriting, postmarks, etc. • Significant transactions undertaken without contacting the customer directly. • Poor security over codes and passwords.

INSURANCE

Management and employee frauds

1 Bogus policies
2 Persuading customers to cancel policies against their interests
3 Forged surrender of policies
4 Misappropriation of funds

External frauds

5 False statements/failure to disclose relevant information
6 Bogus policy holders
7 Staged deaths/accidents/thefts/arson frauds
8 Inflated/false/composite claims
9 Money laundering

Type of fraud	***Examples***	***Warning signs***
Management and employee frauds		
1 Bogus policies	*Doctored capital investment bonds* An insurance agent applied for capital investment bonds from a number of life assurance companies, removed the names, changed the numbers and sold them on to his clients. He insisted that the clients' cheques be made payable to him, leaving investors holding worthless policies. *A sprat to catch a mackerel* Life insurance salesmen forwarded fraudulent policy applications to an insurance company. They paid the first month's premium to give the impression that they were genuine but received in return a much larger amount in initial commission. *Bogus cover notes* A broker issued cover notes for risks which had not been placed on the market with underwriters. The broker pocketed the premiums and forged the underwriters' names on the dealing slips. One of these risks resulted in a claim for £200,000.	• Insurance companies incorporated in remote/offhsore locations with no track record • All dealings through agent; unable to corroborate information given • Abnormally low premiums or favourable terms offered • Abnormal levels of commissions earned

	Non-existent insurance company Four individuals collected premiums on commercial liability policies, performance bonds and financial guarantees for building contractors. They issued policies through an insurance agent in which one of them was an officer, in the name of a non-existent insurance company apparently incorporated in Anguilla. They provided potential policy holders and agents with false financial statements which showed that the insurance company had substantial assets to meet claims.	
2 Persuading customers to cancel policies against their interests	*Too good to be true* An insurance agent induced policy holders to take out new policies, giving them misleading information about interest rates and dividends. However, instead of terminating the old policy he took out loans on them, only later terminating the old policies and rolling over the proceeds into new ones. As a result the policy holders suffered double commission, interest on the loan and lost interest on the money withheld from the new policy.	• Abnormal levels of early policy surrenders. • Unusual trends in commissions.
3 Forged surrender of policies	*Forged signatures* A life insurance agent identified policy holders who had ceased to pay premiums. He then forged the policyholders' signatures on policy surrender documents, sent the documents to head office for processing, requiring the cheques be sent back to him for delivery. On receipt the	• Weak controls over dormant accounts

Type of fraud	*Examples*	*Warning signs*
Management and employee frauds	agent forged endorsements and banked the cheques in his personal account.	
4 Misappropriation of funds	*Defrauding investors* A self-employed life assurance salesman, contracted as an agent for one of the leading insurance companies to sell only their policies, defrauded over 400 investors of their life savings. The investors had invested their life savings in return for a monthly income. The salesman arranged for the monthly income to be paid, misappropriating the larger part of the savings invested. The salesman earned £260,000 in one year selling policies to investors. Although the insurance company did not admit legal responsibility, the company ended up paying very substantial compensations to the victims of the fraud. *Problems with temporary staff* A health insurance company employed a number of temporary staff to clear a backlog of claims. The temporary staff were given authority to pay small claims. One of the temporary members of staff input fictitious claims relating to non-existent dependents of eligible policy holders. Cheques issued were either returned to the individual for despatch so that letters could be attached (most of these cheques were subsequently paid into his	• Unusual trends in commissions earned by particular salesmen. • No independent spot checks of information on claim forms. • Customer complaints/general correspondence not monitored independently.

bank account). In another case he gave his own address as the main address. The individual had perpetrated the same fraud at three other insurance companies previously.

Life savings lost

A company director of a leading life assurance company stole £340,000 from clients to finance his luxurious life style. He met his victims at business seminars, persuading them to hand over large sums of money. He promised to reinvest the money with the life assurance company. However, he paid the money into his own account at a building society.

External frauds

5 False statements/failure to disclose relevant information

False statements and failure to disclose relevant information covers a very wide range of matters, such as age, state of health, previous convictions, financial details, other insurance held, etc.

- Most insurance companies are alert to the risks in this area, using computer-based techniques to identify possible false applications.

6 Bogus policy holders

Men of straw

An individual who ran his own accountancy practice allegedly defrauded insurance companies in respect of pension schemes set up for bogus companies. It was alleged he set up an advisory insurance company to help clients in his accountancy practice. In the course of his accountancy business his clients gave him details of themselves and their families. It was alleged he later used

- Common or like-sounding names between various policy holders.
- No spot checks on information on application forms.
- Unusual trends in payment of premiums.

Type of fraud	***Examples***	***Warning signs***
External frauds	these details when putting forward forged documents to insurance companies. It was also alleged he set up bogus companies and attributed to them bogus employees. He then took out pension schemes for these bogus businesses. In return he received large sums of money by way of insurance commission. The fraud was discovered when an insurance company employee noted that the names of the various companies were very similar and noted that when the accountant was on holiday none of the premiums were paid.	• Incomplete or scrappy documentation accompanying applications.
7 Staged deaths/accidents/ thefts/arson frauds	*Increased premiums but no accidents* An employee of an insurance company bribed the employee of a corporate policy holder to submit false claims. The claims were then misappropriated. The policy holder noted in due course that their insurance premiums had increased due to adverse claims experience although as far as they were aware they had submitted no claims. *Classic smoke* An individual had spent a considerable amount of money in having a classic car restored. He fell on hard times. He arranged for part of the restorer's premises to be set alight. He later submitted a claim to his insurance company for	• As for *Bogus policy* holders • Most insurance companies are alert to the risks in this area and increasingly use sophisticated computer data bases to identify bogus claims

loss of the car, which had been insured at an agreed valuation.

8 Inflated/false/composite claims

These frauds include false claims on life policies, bogus accident claims, arson or otherwise destroying the insured assets and false claims by insurance company employees based on customer policies.

- See *Staged deaths, etc* above

9 Money laundering

Early surrender

Money from drug trafficking was deposited into a number of United Kingdom bank accounts and then transferred to an offshore account. The trafficker entered into a £50,000 life insurance contract, having been introduced by a broking firm. Payment was made by two separate transfers from the offshore account. The funds were represented as the proceeds of overseas investments. At the time of the trafficker's arrest the insurer had received instructions for the early surrender of the contract.

- Payments made from offshore accounts
- Early surrender of contracts

FINANCIAL SECTOR (OTHER FRAUDS)

Mortgage lending

1 Fictitious borrowers/false information on mortgage applications

Leasing

2 Bogus HP agreements/leases for non-existent equipment

Type of fraud	*Examples*	*Warning signs*
Mortgage lending		
1 Fictitious borrowers/false information on mortgage applications	*A jealous mistress . . .* A solicitor defrauded 19 building societies of £4 million. He used his status as a solicitor to apply for mortgages on behalf of bogus house buyers. He borrowed sums ranging from £50,000 to £165,000 for 19 flats and houses around London. Sometimes he obtained loans from up to three separate building societies for the same property. Without registering the loan with the Land Registry his deception was not detected. However, when the building societies tried to trace the borrowers they found that they did not exist because the solicitor had used false names. Five firms of accountants were deceived into producing accounts for fictitious applicants. The solicitor used the funds to lavish extravagant gifts on two mistresses. He also had two houses in London, a villa in Spain and drove a Jaguar and a Cadillac. The police were alerted after one of the building societies indicated that the solicitor had failed to return a mortgage advance after a property deal fell through. The police also received an anonymous phone call, possibly from a jealous mistress who had discovered the existence of a rival. *The Day of the Jackal* An estate agent used a plot from Frederick Forsyth's *The*	• See Lending: *Loans to fictitious borrowers, Impersonation/false information on loan applications* above.

Day of the Jackal to defraud building societies of nearly £500,000. He created a new identity for himself using the name of an infant who died when very young, obtaining the infant's birth certificate and using it as proof of identity. He used this false identity together with a false employer's reference to obtain a mortgage. He also used the identity of his chauffeur and business associate. Sometimes he obtained more than one mortgage on the same property. His wife was a solicitor. Owing to ill health she had allowed her practice to be run partly by her husband who was not qualified to act as a solicitor.

Family of seven make 54 false applications

Several members of a family allegedly made 54 fraudulent mortgage applications, amounting to £1.5 million, over a period of eight years. Many of the mortgages were allegedly obtained by submitting details of fictitious employments, fictitious landlords and false employment references. 19 of the properties relating to the mortgages were used more than once to obtain the mortgages.

128 false applications on more than 90 properties

A group of 19 people, including solicitors, valuers and property developers, made 128 applications for mortgages on more than 90 properties. The applications, with property values falsely inflated by the valuers, were made by the property developers who often used fictitious names. The solicitors colluded in the fraud.

Type of fraud	**Examples**	**Warning signs**
Mortgage lending	*Lord of the Manor (formerly a mini-cab driver)* A mini-cab driver bought the honourary title of Lord of the Manor of Newham. He used the name to apply for bank loans amounting to £2.5 million, helped by four accomplices who included a solicitor, a former magistrate and a mortgage broker. *The financial consultant with a gift for names* A financial consultant obtained mortgages worth £1.38 million. He used fictitious names and obtained surveys that attributed inflated values to the properties. He forged references, contracts, powers of attorney and affidavits to support the bogus applications. *False employment, tenancy details and references* A financial consultant defrauded the UK offshoot of a Canadian bank of £2.2 million by obtaining 30 mortgages using false earnings, employments, tenancy details and references. A surveyor assisted in the fraud by inflating the values of some of the properties involved. *A bright stockbroker* A teenager carried out a series of frauds including obtaining a £466,000 mortgage from a well-known building society.	

During a five-month spending spree he stole his father's American Express gold card running up a bill of £11,000 and ran up a £34,000 bill with a charter jet company. He duped people into believing that he was the youngest qualified stockbroker in London, earning £214,000 a year. Later he persuaded the well-known building society to give him a £466,000 mortgage on a house worth £516,000 in America.

Leasing

2 Bogus HP agreements/ leases for non-existent equipment

Leases on registration numbers

A car dealer financed a lavish lifestyle by defrauding six leading finance companies of more than £5 million. He used friends and family to assist him in a series of bogus hire-purchase deals involving cars which did not exist. He used unused registration numbers of new cars from the licensing centre at Swansea to obtain cash from HP companies, which were in effect paying only for number plates. He then sold the same car with a real registration number to a genuine customer thereby getting paid twice. On one he obtained £110,000 after taking out a phoney hire purchase agreement on a Rolls Royce Silver Spirit.

- No physical inspection of leased asset.
- No direct contact with ultimate customer.
- Abnormal levels of business via particular agents.
- Inconsistencies in documentation.

Cars 'sold' twice

A car dealer sold cars on hire purchase. The customer would sign the relevant documentation which was sent to the hire purchase company for approval. However, often the customer would decide not to proceed with the hire

Type of fraud	Examples	Warning signs
Leasing	purchase agreement and paid cash instead. The dealer accepted the cash and requested the customer to forward the documentation back to him rather than return it to the hire purchase company. The hire purchase company would pay the dealer for the car and he would commence making the repayments in place of the customer. This was repeated many times. Eventually the repayments fell behind and the hire purchase company contacted the original customer at which point the fraud was discovered.	
	Intangible assets	
	The managing director and finance director of a computer equipment company forged signatures of county council customers and entered into leases with leading finance houses for non-existent computer equipment. The company was well-respected and sold Unisys and IBM equipment and had a thriving computer maintenance operation. The directors bought Jaguars and Porches and acquired a company-owned farm. When the company ran into financial difficulties bogus leases were written bearing the forged signatures of the county council customers.	

MONEY LAUNDERING – EXAMPLES OF SUSPICIOUS TRANSACTIONS

Money laundering using cash transactions

- Unusually large cash deposits made by an individual or company whose ostensible business activities would normally be generated by cheques and other instruments.
- Substantial increases in cash deposits of any individual or business without apparent cause, especially if such deposits are subsequently transferred within a short period out of the account and/or to a destination not normally associated with the customer.
- Customers who deposit cash by means of numerous credit slips so that the total of each deposit is unremarkable, but the total of all the credits is significant.
- Company accounts whose transactions, both deposits and withdrawals, are denominated by cash rather than the forms of debit and credit normally associated with commercial operations (e.g., cheques, letters of credit, bills of exchange, etc.).
- Customers who constantly pay in or deposit cash to cover requests for bankers drafts, money transfers or other negotiable and readily marketable money instruments.
- Customers who seek to exchange large quantities of low denomination notes for those of higher denomination.
- Frequent exchange of cash into other currencies.
- Branches that have a great deal more cash transactions than usual. (Head office statistics detect aberrations in cash transactions.)
- Customers whose deposits contain counterfeit notes or forged instruments.
- Customers transferring large sums of money to or from overseas locations with instructions for payment in cash.
- Large cash deposits using night safe facilities, thereby avoiding direct contact with bank or building society staff.

Money laundering using bank or building society accounts

- Customers who wish to maintain a number of trustee or clients' accounts which do not appear consistent with the type of business, including transactions which involve nominee names.
- Customers who have numerous accounts and pay in amounts of cash to each of them in circumstances in which the total of credits would be a large amount.
- Any individual or company whose account shows virtually no normal personal banking or business related activities, but is used to receive or disburse large sums which have no obvious purpose or relationship to the account holder and-or his business (e.g., a substantial increase in turnover on an account).
- Reluctance to provide normal information when opening an account, providing minimal or fictitious information or, when applying to open an account, providing information that is difficult or expensive for the financial institution to verify.
- Customers who appear to have accounts with several financial institutions within the same locality, especially when the bank or building society is aware of a regular consolidation process from such accounts prior to a request for onward transmission of the funds.
- Matching of payments out with credits paid in by cash on the same or previous day.
- Paying in large third party cheques endorsed in favour of the customer.
- Large cash withdrawals from a previously dormant/inactive account, or from an account which has just received an unexpected large credit from abroad.
- Customers who together, and simultaneously, use separate tellers to conduct large cash transactions or foreign exchange transactions.
- Greater use of safe deposit facilities. Increased activity by individuals. The use of sealed packets deposited and withdrawn.
- Companies' representatives avoiding contact with the branch.
- Substantial increases in deposits of cash or negotiable instruments by a professional firm or company, using client accounts or in-house company or trust accounts, especially if the deposits are promptly transferred between other client company and trust accounts.
- Customers who decline to provide information that in normal circumstances would make the customer eligible for credit or for other banking services that would be regarded as valuable.
- Insufficient use of normal banking facilities, e.g., avoidance of high interest rate facilities for large balances.

- Large number of individuals making payments into the same account without an adequate explanation.

Money laundering using investment related transactions

- Purchasing of securities to be held by the financial institution in safe custody, where this does not appear appropriate given the customer's apparent standing.
- Back to back deposits/loan transactions with subsidiaries of, or affiliates of, overseas financial institutions in known drug trafficking areas.
- Requests by customers for investment management services (either foreign currency or securities) where the source of the funds is unclear or not consistent with the customer's apparent standing.
- Larger or unusual settlements of securities in cash form.
- Buying and selling of a security with no discernible purpose or in circumstances which appear unusual.

Money laundering by offshore international activity

- Customer introduced by an overseas branch, affiliate or other bank based in countries where production of drugs or drug trafficking may be prevalent.
- Use of letters of credit and other methods of trade finance to move money between countries where such trade is not consistent with the customer's usual business.
- Customers who make regular and large payments, including wire transactions, that cannot be clearly identified as bona fide transactions to, or receive regular and large payments from countries which are commonly associated with the production, processing or marketing of drugs; proscribed terrorist organisations.
- Building up of large balances, not consistent with the known turnover of the customer's business, and subsequent transfer to account(s) held overseas.
- Unexplained electronic fund transfers by customers on an in and out basis or without passing through an account.
- Frequent requests for travellers cheques, foreign currency drafts or other negotiable instruments to be issued.
- Frequent paying in of travellers cheques or foreign currency drafts particularly if originating from overseas.

Money laundering involving financial institution employees and agents

- Changes in employee characteristics, e.g., lavish lifestyles or avoiding taking holidays.
- Changes in employee or agent performance, e.g., the salesman selling products for cash has remarkable or unexpected increase in performance.
- Any dealing with an agent where the identity of the ultimate beneficiary or counterparty is undisclosed, contrary to normal procedure for the type of business concerned.

Money laundering by secured and unsecured lending

- Customers who repay problem loans unexpectedly.
- Request to borrow against assets held by the financial institution or a third party, where the origin of the assets is not known or the assets are inconsistent with the customer's standing.
- Request by a customer for a financial institution to provide or arrange finance where the source of the customer's financial contribution to a deal is unclear, particularly where property is involved.

FURTHER READING

Fraud: Prevention and Detection by Ian Huntington (Butterworths, 1992).
A textbook covering the risks of fraud and the principles of execution and concealment. Detailed coverage also of the criminal law, the investigation of fraud and fraud prevention.

Corporate Fraud by Michael J Comer (McGraw-Hill, 1977 and 1985).
One of the standard textbooks on corporate fraud.

The Accountant's Handbook of Fraud and Commercial Crime by G Jack Bologna, Robert J Lindquist and Joseph T Wells (John Wiley & Sons Inc, 1993).
An important North American guide on fraud and commercial crime.

Fraudbusting by David Price (Mercury Books, 1991).
A short guide to corporate fraud and fraud prevention.

Fraud. The Growth Industry by Harry West (British Institute of Management, 1988).
A short, entertaining book on fraud by a former senior police officer.

Money Laundering: A practical guide to the new legislation by Rowan Bosworth-Davies and Graham Saltmarsh (Chapman & Hall, 1994).
A very useful guide to recent legislation and to the subject of money laundering generally.

The Money Launderers by Robert Powis (Probus, 1992).
An authoritative American book on the subject of money laundering.

The Laundrymen by Jeffrey Robinson (Simon & Schuster, 1994).
An interesting and wide ranging study of money laundering.

Crime Without Frontiers by Claire Sterling (Little, Brown, 1994).
A fascinating insight into global organised crime.

Aldridge & Parry on *Fraud* by Anthony J Arlidge and Jacques Parry (Waterlow Publishers Ltd, 1985).
One of the standard textbooks on the criminal law.

Serious Fraud: Investigation and Trial by David M Kirk and Anthony JJ Woodcock (Butterworths, 1992).
A major textbook on the prosecution of serious fraud.

Further Reading

Guide to the Financial Services Act 1986 by Barry Rider, Charles Abrams and Ellis Ferrans (CCH 2nd ed., 1989).
A comprehensive guide to the law relating to financial services, including comprehensive treatment of the law relating to insider dealing.

Company Philosophies and Codes of Business Ethics by Simon Webley (Institute of Business Ethics, 1993).
A guide to their drafting and use.

Codes of Business Ethics by Simon Webley (Institute of Business Ethics, 1993).
A checklist and illustrative code.

Index